The Catholic Youth Prayer Book

Mary Shrader, Lauré L. Krupp,
Robert Feduccia Jr.,
and Matthew J. Miller

saint mary's press

Nihil Obstat: Rev. Andrew Beerman, STL
               Censor Librorum
               January 12, 2007

Imprimatur: † Most Reverend Bernard J. Harrington, DD
             Bishop of Winona
             January 12, 2007

The nihil obstat and imprimatur are official declarations that a book or pamphlet is free of doctrinal or moral error. No implication is contained therein that those who have granted the nihil obstat or imprimatur agree with the contents, opinions, or statements expressed, nor do they assume any legal responsibility associated with publication.

The publishing team included Robert Feduccia Jr., development editor; Lorraine Kilmartin, reviewer; prepress and manufacturing coordinated by the production departments of Saint Mary's Press.

Printed in the United States of America

1364 (PO3586)

ISBN 978-1-59982-213-6, leatherette - blue
ISBN 978-0-88489-559-6, leatherette - teal/purple

Contents

Introduction

A Catholic Prayer Book for Teens

Answered Prayer

I asked God for strength, that I might achieve;
I was made weak, that I might learn humbly to obey.
I asked for health, that I might do great things;
I was given sickness, that I might do better things.
I asked for riches, that I might be happy;
I was given poverty, that I might be wise.
I asked for power, that I might have the praise of men;
I was given weakness, that I might feel the need for God.
I asked for all things, that I might enjoy life;
I was given life, that I might enjoy all things.
I received nothing I asked for—but everything I hoped for.
Almost despite myself, my unspoken prayer was answered;
I am, among all men, most richly blessed.

(Unknown Confederate Soldier)

When we talk with God and ask for help, we are in conversation with the one being who has the power to do or change anything. God even has the power to change us.

Sometimes, we ask for God's guidance in a certain way and then find out we have grown differently. Placing our needs and concerns before God allows us to share the struggle with someone loving, accepting—and powerful.

In the process, not only do we find that a situation or problem is better than we thought, but also we are able to see the situation from a new perspective. This is the power and grace of God at work.

When we are able to focus ourselves in prayer, we gain new insights and new perspective and are humbled to embrace God's will in our lives.

Sometimes, in the thick of struggling times, we might feel sorry for ourselves. We might ask God for things that may not really be good for us. For example, "God, please make _____ love me" might be the prayer of a heartbroken person.

Psalm 139:13 tells us that God knew us before we were born. God knows everything about us. Because we do not know all that God knows, it is possible that we don't always ask for what is best—especially if we ask out of pity or selfishness.

Even though our plans might not turn out as we prayed, God surprises us with a wonderful alternative. For example, many young people have prayed to get into a college they had their hearts set on. When they received their rejection letters, they might have thought there was no hope for a good college experience. However, God may have opened a door for them to get into a different school, one that was perfect for them. Their years there were great, and they discovered a major that suited them perfectly.

All of this is part of the wonder of prayer. The most important part of prayer, the goal of prayer, is for us to be shaped in the image of Jesus. Through prayer we can be changed into the image of Jesus to love what he loved as deeply as he loved.

As the Son of God, Jesus knew and experienced the Father intimately. The experience of God as Father is offered to us in prayer. Jesus was love and gave everything he had for others. The process of being changed into love is ours in prayer. God loves us profoundly and wants to give us things. God wants us to ask. God also offers something more for us in prayer. God offers a relationship that fulfills the deepest longing of the human heart.

Imagine it, believe it, and then—*pray!*

You might pray when you are:

- reflecting
- contemplating
- asking or petitioning
- sorrowing
- thankful or grateful
- joyful and praising
- searching or seeking

How to Use This Book

Although prayer is personal in many ways, it is also a community experience. When you pray, God hears you. In addition, all the angels and saints are praying for you and your prayer. Family, friends, and other people you know are united with you in prayer too. Therefore, prayer is ever changing, ever growing, ever evolving.

Because of the community aspect of prayer, some prayers have been handed down for many generations. These traditional prayers may have their origins in the Scriptures, the life of a saint, or a Catholic teaching or other specific person or event.

This book contains a collection of prayers. It includes some traditional prayers for you to pray. It also includes some contemporary and traditional ways to pray, such as an adaptation of the form of prayer known as the Liturgy of the Hours, and journal writing. These options offer you variety in the way you choose to pray. The way you choose to pray might depend on your mood, needs, and energy level.

This book's table of contents gives an overview of the prayers and prayer forms in this book. In addition to the prayers in each chapter, you will also find sidebar notes called Study It!, Pray It!, and Live It!

Study It!

Prayer has a deep history in our Catholic faith and is a rich part of our Tradition. The Study It! sidebar notes help you learn about prayer in general or describe the origins of certain prayers.

Pray It!

Look for ways to be inspired in your own prayer life. Maybe you will discover new ways to pray either individually or with your family, friends, and community.

Live It!

Read about the prayer lives of the saints. People's stories can help us learn more about the value of prayer and can inspire us to live a prayerful life focused on God's will for us. Listen to the lives of others. Think about how you incorporate prayer into your own life.

Pray All Ways

If you have so much as uttered the words "But I don't know how to pray," then you are already on the way to learning how to pray. At the very least, prayer is talking to God, and there is no right or wrong way to do that!

Throughout our lives, we encounter a variety of ways to pray. Certain prayer forms may appeal to us at different times for different reasons.

Examples of types or forms of prayer follow. Ask people you know how they pray, or ask if you can join someone to learn about a form of prayer that is new to you. Browse through *The Catholic Faith Handbook for Youth* (Brian Singer-Towns, Saint Mary's Press, 2004) or another Catholic reference book to learn about these different types of prayer:

- reciting traditional prayers (like the Lord's Prayer)
- meditating
- praying in silence
- singing
- participating in a pilgrimage or prayer walk
- using repetition or mantra (saying one word or phrase over and over)
- talking with God spontaneously
- listening to the sounds of nature
- journal writing
- reading the Scriptures

All ways of prayer are good. Just ask God to guide you, and God will plant the seeds of deeper prayer in your heart.

Tools and Tips

Think about how you like to pray. Look at the following list to see if someplace or something inspires you to live a prayerful life. Consider creating a prayer space, a prayer box, or a prayer journal that contains the information and tools you need to allow yourself the opportunity to pray often.

Consider having more than one of some of these items so you can easily invite a friend, parent, or sibling to pray with you.

- *The Catholic Youth Bible* or another edition of the Bible
- a pen and paper for writing prayers and thoughts
- a cross or crucifix
- a rosary
- a candle
- matches or a lighter (Remember to practice fire safety!)
- prayer cards
- pictures of saints or family members who inspire you
- a prayer shawl or blanket
- a rug or mat
- a small table with a tablecloth
- holy water
- statues or icons of saints
- a small fountain (for the sound of water)
- a chair or other special place to sit or kneel
- flowers or other items from nature
- this book, other books, and resources that include prayers and writings that inspire you personally
- music (a CD and a CD player or musical instrument)
- art supplies, such as markers, paints, clay, chalk, and paper
- a special item, such as your own baptismal candle or a grand-parent's rosary
- a missalette or other publication that lists the weekly readings

Your Comments or Suggestions

Saint Mary's Press wants to know your reactions to the materials in this book. We are open to all kinds of suggestions from young people and want to continue to provide resources that enliven your hearts and minds with the Good News of Jesus Christ. Please let us know how we can help you pray all ways.

If you have a comment or suggestion, please write to us at 702 Terrace Heights, Winona, MN 55987-1318, or send an e-mail to *smp@smp.org.*

Part I

Prayers for Today's Teenagers

Chapter 1
Prayers for Living

Prayers to Seek God's Presence
in the Events of Life

It's Hard to See You Some Days, Jesus

To Jesus, the Good Shepherd:
Open my eyes,
that I might see your glorious
   light.
Open my mind,
that I may know your truth.
Open my heart,
   that I might receive your
   healing touch.
And open my ears,
   that I might hear you say,
"I love you."
Amen.

A Simple Prayer

O God:
Open my ears to hear you
and my heart to receive you,
and strengthen my will
that I may follow you.
Amen.

Living True

Jesus:
Sometimes I know exactly what
   you want me to do,
but I don't have the courage to
   do it.
I am tired of being this way.
Help me stand up straight
and be who you made me to
   be—
Strong, confident, and unafraid.
Amen.

Being Left Out by Friends

To Jesus, on the cross:
You know what hurt is
and how it feels
to be left behind by your friends.
You know how I feel,
and I know how you felt.
I will stay with you today,
and I know that you will stay
   with me.
Amen.

Joyful Hearts, Give Praise!

What does praising God mean? We know how to thank God. We know how to ask God for things. We know how to ask God to forgive us. We know how to pray. But what does praising God mean?

Giving thanks is about acknowledging what God *does;* giving praise is about acknowledging who God *is.* The root of the word *praise* also gives us the word *prize.* What do you prize about God?

Who is God? How have you experienced God? Some like to think of God's loving nature. Others like to think of God as a friend who never leaves their side. You may prize God's constancy. No matter how many things change in your life, God remains the same. What do you love about God?

Make a list of things you prize about God. This list is your own litany of praise. Read your list and make it your prayer. Before each thing you prize, say, "I praise you, God, for . . ." This will become your prize, your gift to God.

There Is So Much

To Jesus, who calmed the stormy
    sea:
There is so much pressure,
there is so much hurt,
there is so much confusion,
there is so much noise.
    Jesus, please calm this storm,
so that I may
sit peacefully in this boat with
    you.
Amen.

I Don't Have Much, Lord

To Jesus, who knew a treasure
when he saw one:
Some thought money was the
    treasure,
but you found a treasure
in the two copper coins
a poor widow offered.
I don't have much, Lord,
but what I have is yours.
I know that when I give you
    myself,
my offering
becomes your treasure.
Amen.

I Need You, God

To the God who loves me:
As I reach up to you today,
will you reach down to meet me?
I'm counting on it.
Amen.

Stress

To God, who made everything:
You made the earth and every-
    thing on it.
You made the heavens and every-
    thing in it.
I know you can handle the stress
    I am facing.
I will keep my heart open today,
so I can feel your power at work
    in me.
Amen.

I Can't Do Anything Right

God:
It feels like I can't do anything
    right,
like I got up in a parallel universe
    or something.
Help me remember today that
    wherever I am,
you are there,
and that your love for me doesn't
    depend on what I do.
You love me just because I am.
Amen.

God Is Light

Loving God:
Take away the darkness
and fill me with the radiant light
of your Son, Jesus Christ.
Amen.

Boyfriend or Girlfriend Trouble

To Jesus, who promised to carry
    my burdens:
I have a broken heart,
and I have to live with it
while I deal with homework,
friends,
and everything else.
Lord Jesus,
will you carry my heavy heart?
Will your love fill the empty
    space
that was left when that love was
    taken from me?
Amen.

Why Did You Let It Happen, God?

I don't get it,
and I don't get you.
Why did you let it happen?
I don't understand. . . .
But even while I am mad at you,
I still feel hope inside me.
I trust you,
even though I don't know why.
I guess that deep down, I know
you will help me through.
I choose to believe in you
in the middle of it all.
Amen.

It's a Great Day

To the God of glory:
Thank you, God,
for all you have given me,
for everything that makes today
    great—
the tangible things
and this good feeling I have
but can't explain.
Amen.

Confused

To Jesus, who is the light of the
    world
and the light of my world too:
No matter how dark the dark-
    ness is,
your light is shining.
Help me keep my eyes on your
    light
and not on the darkness that
    swarms around me.
I don't know what your plan for
    me is, Lord,
but I know you have one.
Help me hang on
until the time is right
for you to show it to me.
Amen.

Growing Closer to God

When we think of growing, we usually think of moving up. Plants become taller when they grow. A promotion at work means a step up on the ladder.

Growing closer to God is all about going deeper, not about moving up.

"I will put my law within them, and I will write it on their hearts; and I will be their God, and they shall be my people" (Jer. 31:33).

To grow closer to God, we must go to the depth of our hearts, where God's law is written, where God dwells. We don't have to put something into our hearts; rather, we must learn to listen to that place in our hearts where God's law is written. The more we listen, the easier hearing God becomes.

"Baptism seals the Christian with the indelible spiritual mark *(character)* of his belonging to Christ" (*Catechism of the Catholic Church,* no. 1272).

You were forever changed when you were baptized. When the mark of Jesus Christ was engraved onto your soul, you received a homing device of sorts that leads you back to God—if you listen.

Think of sunflowers. They are unusual by almost any measure. They are taller, stronger, and bigger than most flowers. Of course, the most fascinating aspect of sunflowers is that they follow the sun as it makes its way across the sky. They do this even on cloudy days. Somehow, they just do it.

As the sunflowers follow the sun, so does your heart follow God. Sin may sometimes prevent you from turning toward God, but the key is to learn to listen to your heart—to go to the depths where God's word is written, where the mark of your Baptism is found. Here you will learn to grow in virtue.

Saint Cecilia

Imagine walking though an underground tunnel, a seemingly endless maze of small rooms and nooks. It is damp and cold, and though there are lamps, you cannot help but feel the darkness of the place.

Your thoughts turn to the people who first dug these tunnels, called catacombs. The diggers were the Christians during the time that Christianity was illegal in Rome, a time when being a Christian could get a person killed. The Christians of those days hid in these tunnels for meetings, for celebrating the Eucharist, and for fellowship.

You come to a room a bit larger than the others. There you see a sculpture of Saint Cecilia that was created ages ago. The room is filled with vibrantly colored murals of her. Everything about this room says Cecilia was unique.

Cecilia was a noblewoman of her time who gave up everything for her faith. After the Roman authorities martyred her husband and his brother for their Christian faith, Cecilia brought their bodies to her estate and buried them there. For this the authorities sentenced Cecilia to die. She lived for three days after an executioner attempted to behead her. During that time, Cecilia used her worldly goods to take care of people who were poor, made provisions to leave her home to the Christian Church, and continued to sing praises to God. That is part of the reason she is the patron saint of singers. Even through the painful wounds of an executioner, Cecilia gave praise.

In the pains and sufferings of life, Cecilia can inspire us always to have hearts that are joyful and focused on the Lord.

My Dream Is Shattered

To the loving God
who cares about my dreams:
Bless and restore me.
In my disappointment and
    sadness,
help me remember
that you have a future full of
    hope for me.
Give me a new dream.
Amen.

I Want to Be Close to You, God

Lord Jesus:
I want to see you.
I want to know you.
I want to follow you.
I want to know your will for me,
so I may do it.
I love you.
Amen.

God Has a Plan for Me

Loving God:
Fill me with confidence and trust
that in knowing your will, I may
    follow it,
and that in following your will,
I will find joy.
Amen.

I Have Faith

To Jesus Christ, my Lord:
I can't explain it, Lord,
but today I know you are with
    me.
I know you hold me
in the palm of your hand.
I know you love me
and will guide me.
I know there is nothing
you can't do.
I know there is nothing
you won't do
for me.
Amen.

I'm Sorry, God

To Jesus, who forgave Peter
for denying him three times:
Please give me the guts
to be honest with myself.
Give me the humility
to admit my sins.
And give me wisdom
so I will know how to repair the
    harm I have caused.
Forgive me, Lord,
for what I have done,
and give me grace
not to do it again.
Amen.

I Want to Do Good Work in the World

To the Lord
who calls me to great things:
You have created me good.
In my Baptism, you placed
    within me
the same Spirit
that raised Christ Jesus from the
    dead.
Help me, Lord,
to open my heart
and let the good that you have
    placed in me
flow out into the world.
Amen.

Chapter 2
Prayers Through the Day

Prayers to Seek God's Presence
Through the Day

Morning Prayers

Hymn for Sunday Morning: "*Te Deum*" ("You Are God")

You are God: we praise you;
You are the Lord: we acclaim you;
You are the eternal Father:
All creation worships you.
To you all angels, all the powers
    of heaven,
Cherubim and Seraphim, sing in
    endless praise:
    Holy, holy, holy, Lord, God of
    power and might, heaven and
    earth are full of your glory.
The glorious company of apostles
    praise you.
The noble fellowship of prophets
    praise you.
The white-robed army of martyrs
    praise you.
Throughout the world the holy
    Church acclaims you:

Father, of majesty unbounded,
your true and only Son, worthy
    of all worship,
    and the Holy Spirit, advocate
    and guide.
You, Christ, are the king of glory,
the eternal Son of the Father.
When you became man to set us
    free
you did not spurn the Virgin's
    womb.
You overcame the sting of death,
and opened the kingdom of heav-
    en to all believers.
You are seated at God's right
    hand in glory.
We believe that you will come,
    and be our judge.
Come then, Lord, and help your
    people,
bought with the price of your own
    blood,
and bring us with your saints
to glory everlasting.

Ignatian Examination of Conscience

Saint Ignatius of Loyola wanted to be fully present to God throughout his day. To prepare for the next day, he reviewed the day he had just lived. This review, or examination, brought to mind ways he was present to God and ways he needed to be more present to God.

Before you go to bed at night, take a little time to end your day with God. This will help you let go of the day and start tomorrow fresh—a clean slate, a new beginning. Following are several ways to do so:

- Begin by thanking God for the day.
- Ask the Holy Spirit to help you see the day through his eyes.
- Think through your day, hour by hour. Getting out of bed and ready for school . . . arriving at school and seeing your friends . . . going through your morning classes . . . lunch . . . afternoon classes . . . after-school activities . . . coming home . . .
- What are you grateful for? When did you see God working? For those moments, pray, "Thank you, God, for . . ."
- What are you sorry for? Everyone sins. The greatest damage, however, isn't in the moment of the act itself but is in the effects the act has on others, ourselves, and our relationship with God. We can feel shameful, or we may think we are bad people. It is much better simply to acknowledge our sins and shortcomings and to ask God and others to forgive us.
- After your have contemplated your day, ask God to help you grow closer to God.
- Last, ask God to guard you while you sleep, to keep your heart and mind fixed on God, and to help you wake up ready to serve throughout another day.

Psalm 33:20–22

Our soul waits for the LORD;
   he is our help and shield.
Our heart is glad in him, because
   we trust in his holy name.
Let your steadfast love, O LORD,
   be upon us,
even as we hope in you.

Take This Day

To Jesus, who changed the water
   into wine:
Take this day
and make it into something
   beautiful.
Amen.

The Morning Offering

O Jesus,
through the Immaculate Heart
   of Mary,
I offer You my prayers, works,
joys and sufferings
of this day for all the intentions
of Your Sacred Heart,
in union with the Holy Sacrifice
   of the Mass
throughout the world,
in reparation for my sins,
for the intentions of all my
   relatives and friends,
and in particular for the intentions of the Holy Father.
Amen.

A True Friend to Jesus

To Jesus, who called us friends:
Let me be a true friend to you
   today.
Let my words and my actions
Tell the world how much I love
   you.
Amen.

Prayers at School

Prayer Before a Test

Lord:
I have studied, but there is so
   much to remember.
Please give me a clear mind.
Please keep distractions away
   from me.
Do not allow the pressure of the
   moment to frustrate me.
Help me instead to calmly take
   this test
with the confidence that you will
   help me
remember everything I have
   studied.
Amen.

Sanctifying the Day

To sanctify means to set something aside for holiness. Just how do you sanctify your day, or make it holy?

God makes things holy!

To set your day aside for God, simply recognize that you are in God's presence constantly. God is already there and is already aware of what is happening with you. Remember this. Turn to God and say yes.

The film *The Prince of Egypt* (1998, 90 minutes, rated PG) is the animated story of God's calling Moses to lead the Hebrews out of Egypt. At the burning bush, Moses draws near and hears God calling his name: "Moses! Moses!" Moses cannot see the person calling, but the voice becomes like a wind whirling around him. Moses finds himself lifted off his feet by the power of this call.

Think of God's presence in your life as being like that wind. It is constantly around us. God's presence and call to us are as real as the air we breathe. We cannot see air. Yet, though it is invisible, though it is most often forgotten, air is still real. It still gives us life.

In the middle of a busy day, remembering God can be hard. But God doesn't go away when we don't think about God. God is all around us, like the air we breathe.

Use a reminder that will help you remember to turn to God, perhaps every time the bell rings if you are at school. Pray: "Thank you, God, for being with me. Help me stay near you as I continue my day."

Connect your day with God. Make it, and yourself, holy.

Prayer After a Test

Lord:
I worry about my grades.
It is very easy for me to obsess
    over a test
I am going to take and tests I
    have taken.
I give you my concerns about
the test I have just taken.
I ask that the teacher grade it
    fairly,
and I ask that I go about the rest
    of the day
with confidence that I did my
    best.
Amen.

Prayer for Holy Words

Merciful Jesus:
It is very easy for me to join my
    friends
when someone is being talked
    about,
when the conversation is
about something inappropriate,
or when the language becomes
    coarse.
Give me the right words when
the wrong words are being used.
May my words be only those that
    will bless others,
not hurt or offend them.
Amen.

Prayers at Meals

Prayer Before Meals

Bless us, O Lord, and these
your gifts, which we are about
to receive from your bounty,
through Christ, our Lord.
Amen.

Prayer After Meals

We give you thanks for all your
benefits almighty God,
who lives and reigns forever
and ever.
Amen.

Prayers at Midday

Psalm 19:14

Let the words of my mouth and
        the meditation of my heart
    be acceptable to you,
    O Lord, my rock and my
        redeemer.

You Are Near

Lord:
Keep me mindful of your love,
and help me remember that you
    are near.
Amen.

Saint Ignatius of Loyola

Saint Ignatius of Loyola is an inspiration to all who have been confused about what they should do with their life or what God calls them to, or perhaps to those who think they are following God but then get turned around.

Ignatius began life as, well, a partier. He was rich and popular and hung out at the royal court with all the other rich and popular people. But he was also a soldier. After being hit by a cannonball in battle, Ignatius was laid up for quite a while. The only books around were those about Christ and the lives of the saints. With nothing else to do, Ignatius began reading. These stories stirred his soul to the point that he committed himself to a life of faith and virtue.

Exactly what that meant, however, wasn't clear. Ignatius decided to travel to the Holy Land, which is modern-day Israel and surrounding areas. After a long and difficult journey, he arrived, only to be told he had to leave. He often suffered from poverty and bad health and was the victim of rumor campaigns.

Years after his injury, Ignatius gradually began to understand God's way. Eventually, Ignatius founded a religious order called the Society of Jesus, also known as the Jesuits. Ignatius centered the life of his order on a love for Jesus that was lived every moment of the day. He challenged the other Jesuits to become aware of God's calling in the small things. He instructed his followers to stop at moments through the day and to be aware of how they were saying yes to God.

Psalm 23

The LORD is my shepherd, I shall
    not want.
  He makes me lie down in
  green pastures;
he leads me beside still waters;
  he restores my soul.
He leads me in right paths
  for his name's sake.

Even though I walk through the
    darkest valley,
  I fear no evil;
for you are with me;
  your rod and your staff—
  they comfort me.

You prepare a table before me
  in the presence of my enemies;
you anoint my head with oil;
  my cup overflows.
Surely goodness and mercy shall
    follow me
  all the days of my life,
and I shall dwell in the house of
    the LORD
  my whole life long.

Night Prayers

Night Prayer Antiphon

Protect us, Lord, as we stay
  awake; watch over us as we
  sleep,
that awake, we may keep watch
  with Christ, and asleep,
rest in his peace.
Amen.

Psalm 141:1–4

I call upon you, O LORD; come
    quickly to me;
  give ear to my voice when I
  call to you.
Let my prayer be counted as
    incense before you,
  and the lifting up of my hands
  as an evening sacrifice.

Set a guard over my mouth, O
    LORD;
  keep watch over the door of
  my lips.
Do not turn my heart to any evil,
  to busy myself with wicked
  deeds
in company with those who work
    iniquity;
  do not let me eat of their
  delicacies.

Canticle of Simeon: Luke 2:29–32

"Master, now you are dismissing
　　your servant in peace,
　according to your word;
for my eyes have seen your
　　salvation,
　which you have prepared in
　the presence of all peoples,
a light for revelation to the
　　Gentiles
　and for glory to your people
　Israel."

While I Sleep

Lord God:
I know that you can be at work,
even while I sleep.
Keep my heart and mind on you.
Heal me of injury,
make my heart strong,
make my soul pure,
and may I grow closer to you.
Amen.

Part II

Prayers from the Catholic Tradition

Chapter 3
Marian Prayers

Prayers and Devotions to Mary,
the Mother of God

Hail Mary

Hail Mary, full of grace,
the Lord is with you!
Blessed you are among women,
and blessed is the fruit of your
  womb, Jesus.
Holy Mary, Mother of God,
pray for us sinners
now and at the hour of our
  death.

The Oldest Marian Prayer: "*Sub Tuum Praesidium*" (Under Your Protection)

We fly to your patronage, O
  Holy Mother of God. Despise
  not our petitions in our necessities but deliver us always
  from all dangers, O glorious
  and blessed Virgin.

The Angelus

The Angelus is traditionally recited morning (6:00 a.m.), noon, and evening (6:00 p.m.). Monks pray Morning Prayer, Midday Prayer, and Evening Prayer. By praying at set times of the day, the entire day is made holy. In the Middle Ages, the local churches' bells rang at these set times, and the laypeople stopped their work, gathered in small groups of two or more, and prayed the Angelus as a way to make their day holy. The Angelus can be said either in a group or alone.

Beads and Mantras

Throughout the world's many religions, including Catholicism, *mantras* have an important place in prayer and meditation. A mantra is a word or phrase that one repeats while meditating. The repetition occupies the body and allows the mind and spirit to pray more completely. When praying the rosary, the Hail Marys become a mantra.

Beads are also used in other world religions besides Catholicism. For example, Muslims use a set of ninety-nine beads. Each bead represents a name for God in the Islamic faith. These beads become a kind of mantra for the hands.

In praying the rosary, the beads help one keep count of the Our Fathers and Hail Marys. But the beads also help the person engage the entire body in prayer. Through the repetition of the mantra and the handling of the beads, a person's body, mind, and spirit are active and can enter more deeply into the mysteries of Jesus's life.

Leader: The Angel of the Lord declared unto Mary,

Response: And she conceived of the Holy Spirit.

All: Hail Mary . . .

Leader: Behold the handmaid of the Lord,

Response: Be it done unto me according to your word.

All: Hail Mary . . .

Leader: And the Word was made flesh,

Response: And dwelt among us.

All: Hail Mary . . .

Leader: Pray for us, O holy Mother of God,

Response: That we may be made worthy of the promises of Christ.

Leader: Let us pray: Pour forth, we beseech you, O Lord, your grace into our hearts that we to whom the incarnation of Christ, your Son, was made known by the message of an angel may, by his passion and cross, be brought to the glory of his resurrection, through Christ our Lord.

(Adapted from Brian Singer-Towns, *The Catholic Faith Handbook for Youth,* p. 381)

Hail, Holy Queen

Hail, holy Queen, mother of mercy, our life, our sweetness, and our hope.

To you do we cry, poor banished children of Eve.

To you do we send up our sighs, mourning and weeping in this vale of tears.

Turn then, most gracious advocate,
your eyes of mercy toward us,
and after this our exile show
to us the blessed fruit of your womb, Jesus.

O clement, O loving,
O sweet Virgin Mary.

"Memorare" (Remember, O Most Gracious Virgin Mary)

Remember, O most gracious Virgin Mary, that never was it known that anyone who fled to your protection, implored your help or sought your intercession was left unaided. Inspired with confidence, I fly to you, O virgin of virgins, my Mother. To you I come, before you I stand, sinful and sorrowful. O Mother of the Word Incarnate, despise not my petitions, but in your mercy, hear and answer me. Amen.

"Novena to Our Lady of Perpetual Help"

A novena is a process of praying for nine consecutive periods of time (typically nine days in a row). If something particular is on someone's mind or heart, that person may seek the prayers of Our Lady of Perpetual Help by praying these prayers for nine days.

Give your loving gaze to me, Our Lady of Perpetual Help. I am a person who wants to follow your Son, Jesus, but find it difficult. I come to you for comfort and help.

O Mother of Mercy, come to my aid. I hear that you are called the refuge and the hope of sinners and the weak. Be my refuge and my hope.

Help me, for the love of Jesus Christ. Stretch out your hand to take me by the hand and guide me to your Son. I simply and humbly entrust myself to your prayers and help. I bless and thank Almighty God, who in God's mercy has given me this confidence in you.

Mary, tender Mother, help me. Mother of Perpetual Help, may I always keep my eyes on Jesus and follow him with all my heart. Amen.

Pray the Lord's Prayer, Hail Mary, and Glory Be, three times each.

Easter Hymn to Mary: *"Regina Coeli"* ("Queen of Heaven")

Queen of heaven, rejoice, alleluia.
The Son whom you merited to bear, alleluia,
has risen as he said, alleluia.
Rejoice and be glad, O Virgin Mary, alleluia!
For the Lord has truly risen, alleluia.

The Rosary

Twenty mysteries are reflected upon in the rosary: five joyful mysteries, five luminous mysteries, five sorrowful mysteries, and five glorious mysteries. As suggested by Pope John Paul II, the joyful mysteries are said on Monday and Saturday, the luminous on Thursday, the sorrowful on Tuesday and Friday, and the glorious on Wednesday and Sunday (with these exceptions: on Sundays of the Christmas season, the joyful mysteries are prayed; and on Sundays of the Lenten season, the sorrowful mysteries are prayed).

The History of the Rosary

The word *rosary* quickly calls to mind the image of roses. This is the actual origin of the word. The rosary is seen as a bouquet of roses for Mary, the Mother of God. Although the origin of the word is easy to identify, the history is a bit more complex.

To understand the rosary, the place of the Psalms should first be explained. The 150 Psalms constituted the prayer book of Jews, Jesus, and the early Christians. One group of these Christians was monks. With the Psalms as their prayer book, many communities of monks committed themselves to praying all of the Psalms within the span of a month, a week, or even a day. Before the introduction of the luminous mysteries in 2002, the entire rosary consisted of 150 Hail Marys, just as there are 150 Psalms. By meditating on the life of Jesus and by praying 150 Hail Marys, the Christians who lived and worked in the world had a way to join the monks in their constant praise of God.

Saint Louis de Montfort

Louis Mary Grignion de Montfort was born to a poor family on January 31, 1673, at Montfort, France, and was ordained to the priesthood in 1700.

Eventually Saint Louis went to Rome, where Pope Clement XI appointed him a missionary in a part of France known as Brittany. Louis was known for his impassioned preaching and his ability to draw people into a deep devotion to Mary. He also wrote a very popular book, *True Devotion to the Blessed Virgin.* In 1715 Louis organized several priests and formed the Missionaries of the Company of Mary. He died in 1716. In 1947 Pope Pius XII canonized him.

The spiritual legacy of Louis has had a lasting impact on the Church. In recent times, Pope John Paul II had a very deep love for Mary. In fact, at one point in his life, he wondered if his devotion to Mary was excessive. Was his love for Mary crowding out his love for Jesus? The Pope found his answer in the words of Louis. In *True Devotion to the Blessed Virgin,* the Holy Father found that his devotion was not excessive. Louis said that true devotion to the Blessed Mother always leads to a greater intimacy with the Lord Jesus.

Words from Saint Francis de Sales

Do Not Look to Tomorrow

Do not look forward to what may happen tomorrow. The same Everlasting Father, who takes care of you today, will take care of you tomorrow, and every day. He will either shield you from suffering or give you unfailing strength to bear it. Be at peace, then, and put aside all anxious thoughts and imaginations!

The Everlasting God has in His wisdom foreseen from eternity the cross He now presents to you as a gift from His inmost Heart. This cross He now sends you He has considered with His all-knowing eyes, understood with His divine mind, tested with His wise justice, warmed with loving arms and weighed with His own Hands, to see that it be not one inch too large and not one ounce too heavy for you. He has blessed it with His Holy Name, anointed it with His grace, perfumed it with His consolation, taken one last glance at you and your courage, and then sent it to you from heaven, a special greeting from God to you, an alms of the all-merciful love of God.

Prayer of Saint Catherine of Siena

Lord, take me from myself and give me to yourself.

Three Prayers of Saint Ignatius of Loyola

Take, O Lord, and Receive

Take, O Lord, and receive my entire liberty, my memory, my understanding and my whole will. All that I am and all that I possess You have given me: I surrender it all to You to be disposed of according to Your will. Give me only Your love and Your grace; with these I will be rich enough, and will desire nothing more. Amen.

Grant, O Lord, That My Heart

Grant, O Lord, that my heart may neither desire nor seek anything but what is necessary for the fulfillment of Thy holy Will. May health or sickness, riches or poverty, honors or contempt, humiliations, leave my soul in that state of perfect detachment to which I desire to attain for Thy greater honor and Thy greater glory. Amen.

O My God, Teach Me

O my God, teach me to be generous:
to serve you as you deserve to be served;
to give without counting the cost;
to fight without fear of being wounded;
to work without seeking rest;
and to spend myself without expecting any reward,
but the knowledge that I am doing your holy will.

Prayer of Saint Gertrude the Great

Fire of God

O ardent fire of my God, which contains, produces, and imprints those living ardors which attract the humid waters of my soul, and dry up the torrents of earthly delights, and afterwards soften my hard self-opinionatedness, which time has hardened so exceedingly!

O consuming fire, which even amid ardent flames imparts sweetness and peace to the soul! In thee, and in none other, do we receive this grace of being reformed to the image and likeness in which we were created.

O burning furnace, in which we enjoy the true vision of peace, which tries and purifies the gold of the elect, and leads the soul to seek eagerly for its highest good, even thyself, in thy eternal truth.

Relics

After a friend or family member has died, many people continue to visit the grave of that person or cherish one of the person's belongings—a ring, a scarf, a journal. Those visits and possessions keep our memory of that person alive in our hearts. We would certainly not forget a person without those items, but they do help us feel connected to those who have died and can help us embody the qualities we admired.

A relic is an actual item from a saint. This could include an article of clothing, a personal item, or even his or her remains, such as bones. Sometimes, relics of a saint are kept in special churches or other places people can visit.

The earliest Christians went to the graves of those who were martyred because of their love for Jesus. It was a way to honor their sacrifice and also a prayer that the living Christians would have the same virtue and love for Jesus that the martyrs possessed.

Saint Perpetua

About AD 202, the Roman authorities imprisoned Saint Perpetua for being a Christian. When she was arrested, she was preparing to be baptized. Even though not yet baptized, she refused to denounce her faith. She prayerfully considered that she would not survive if she continued to proclaim her belief in Jesus Christ. Her heartbroken father urged her to deny her faith. She simply refused.

Perpetua knew that God would not leave her side. She placed her trust in God and accepted the Romans' punishment for being a Christian. By turning to God wholeheartedly, she was filled with peace and joy even in the midst of torture. God gave her the strength to endure terrible things by helping her to focus on God's love for her.

After having her children taken from her, Perpetua was sent to the wild beasts in front of roaring crowds. She died at the age of 22.

Martyrs like Perpetua believe their faith is worth dying for so we will know that our faith is worth living for!

Prayer of Saint Padre Pio
A Prayer After Communion

Stay with me, Lord, for it is necessary to have You present so that I do not forget You. You know how easily I abandon You.

Stay with me, Lord, because I am weak and I need Your strength, that I may not fall so often.

Stay with me, Lord, for You are my life, and without You, I am without fervor.

Stay with me, Lord, for You are my light, and without You, I am in darkness.

Stay with me, Lord, to show me Your will.

Stay with me, Lord, so that I hear Your voice and follow You.

Stay with me, Lord, for I desire to love You very much, and always be in Your company.

Stay with me, Lord, if You wish me to be faithful to You.

Stay with me, Lord, for as poor as my soul is, I wish it to be a place of consolation for You, a nest of Love.

Stay with me, Jesus, for it is getting late and the day is coming to a close, and life passes, death, judgement, eternity approaches. It is necessary to renew my strength, so that I will not stop along the way and for that, I need You. It is getting late and death approaches. I fear the darkness, the temptations, the dryness, the cross, the sorrows. O how I need You, my Jesus, in this night of exile!

Stay with me tonight, Jesus, in life with all its dangers, I need You.

Let me recognize You as Your disciples did at the breaking of bread, so that the Eucharistic Communion be the light which disperses the darkness, the force which sustains me, the unique joy of my heart.

Stay with me, Lord, because at the hour of my death, I want to remain united to You, if not by Communion, at least by grace and love.

Stay with me, Jesus, I do not ask for divine consolation, because I do not merit it, but, the gift of Your Presence, oh yes, I ask this of You!

Stay with me, Lord, for it is You alone I look for. Your Love, Your Grace, Your Will, Your Heart, Your Spirit, because I love You and ask no other reward but to love You more and more.

With a firm love, I will love You with all my heart while on earth and continue to love You perfectly during all eternity. Amen.

The Prayer of Saint Francis of Assisi

O Lord, make me an instrument of your peace.
Where there is hatred, let me sow love;
where there is injury, pardon;
where there is doubt, faith;
where there is despair, hope;
where there is darkness, light;
where there is sadness, joy.

O Divine Master, grant that I may not so much seek to be consoled as to console;
to be understood as to understand;
to be loved as to love.

For it is in giving that we receive;
it is in pardoning that we are pardoned;
and it is in dying that we are born to eternal life. Amen.

Prayer of Saint Augustine of Hippo

Prayer to the Holy Spirit

Breathe in me, O Holy Spirit, that my thoughts may all be holy.
Act in me, O Holy Spirit, that my work, too, may be holy.
Draw my heart, O Holy Spirit, that I love but what is holy.
Strengthen me, O Holy Spirit, to defend all that is holy.
Guard me, then, O Holy Spirit, that I always may be holy.
Amen.

Chapter 5
Devotional Prayers

Devotions and Prayers
for a Specific Purpose

Prayer to the Holy Spirit

Come, Holy Spirit, fill the hearts of your faithful. Enkindle in them the fire of your love. Send forth your Spirit and they will be created. And you will renew the face of the earth.

Lord, by the light of the Holy Spirit, you have taught the hearts of the faithful. In the same Spirit, help us relish what is right and always rejoice in your consolation. We ask this through Christ, our Lord. Amen.

Chaplet of the Divine Mercy

Similar to the rosary, a chaplet is a series of repeated prayers in which a string of beads is used. Early in the twentieth century, a humble Polish woman received visions of

Jesus. In those visions, Jesus spoke to her about his mercy and his desire to give mercy. The following chaplet flows from those visions and is given to advance the three reasons for the visions: to give God's mercy, to urge us to be merciful, and to urge all people to trust in Jesus. This prayer uses rosary beads and begins in the following manner:

- *Make the sign of the cross.*
- *Pray the Lord's Prayer.*
- *Pray the Hail Mary.*
- *Pray the Apostles' Creed.*

On the single bead before each decade, say:

Eternal Father, I offer You the Body and Blood, Soul and Divinity of Your dearly beloved Son, Our Lord Jesus Christ, in atonement for our sins and those of the whole world.

For the sake of His sorrowful Passion, have mercy on us and on the whole world.

After praying the five decades, conclude by repeating three times:

Holy God, Holy Mighty One, Holy Immortal One,
    have mercy on us and on the whole world.
Amen.

Prayer Before a Crucifix

Look down upon me, good and gentle Jesus, while before Your face I humbly kneel and, with burning soul, pray and beseech You to fix deep in my heart lively sentiments of faith, hope, and charity; true contrition for my sins; and a firm purpose of amendment.

While I contemplate, with great love and tender pity, Your five most precious wounds, ponder over them within me and calling to mind the words which David, Your prophet, said to You, my Jesus:

"They have pierced My hands and My feet, they have numbered all My bones."

Act of Consecration to the Holy Spirit

I pray to you, God the Holy Spirit, and I give all of myself to you. I worship you for you are pure, just, and powerful as love. You are my strength. You are my guide. I ask for you to surround me and change me. Change my mind to think like Jesus. Change my body to act like Jesus. Change my heart to love like Jesus. Give me the ears to hear your voice guiding me, and when I hear your voice, may I obey. Make me holy and joyful. Give me the courage I need to live as a missionary. May people come to know Jesus because I am in their lives.

Amen.

Prayer for the Seven Gifts of the Holy Spirit

Christ Jesus, before ascending into heaven, You promised to send the Holy Spirit to Your apostles and disciples. Grant that the same Spirit may perfect in our lives the work of Your grace and love.

Grant us:

- **The Spirit of Fear of the Lord** that we may be filled with a loving reverence toward You;
- **The Spirit of Piety** that we may find peace and fulfillment in the service of God while serving others;
- **The Spirit of Fortitude** that we may bear our cross with You and, with courage, overcome the obstacles that interfere with our salvation;
- **The Spirit of Knowledge** that we may know You and know ourselves and grow in holiness;
- **The Spirit of Understanding** to enlighten our minds with the light of Your truth;
- **The Spirit of Counsel** that we may choose the surest way of doing Your will, seeking first the Kingdom;
- **The Spirit of Wisdom** that we may aspire to the things that last forever; Teach us to be Your faithful disciples and animate us in every way with Your Spirit.

Amen.

Novena to the Holy Spirit

Follow this course of prayer for nine days:

First Day: Creation Awaits Fulfillment

Holy Spirit, Lord of light! From Your clear celestial height, Your pure beaming radiance give!

Almighty and eternal God, send forth Your Spirit, who brought order from chaos at the beginning of the universe, and peace to the Lord's disciples.

Grant that I, as your creation, baptized in your Spirit, may be filled with the seven gifts so that I may forever do your will and renew the face of the earth.

Amen.

Pray the Lord's Prayer, the Hail Mary, and the Glory Be.

Second Day: Christ's Promise to Send the Paraclete

Come, Father of the poor! Come, treasures which endure! Come, Light of all that live!

Come, O Blessed Spirit of Holy Fear, fill me with devotion to God alone.

In the Risen Christ, I welcome You, O Spirit of truth, whom the Father sends in Jesus's name.

Wash clean the sinful soul, and rain down your grace that we may be one with the Church in fidelity to our Lord, Jesus Christ.

Amen.

Pray the Lord's Prayer, the Hail Mary, and the Glory Be.

Third Day: The Soul of Christ's Body, the Church

Thou, of all consolers, best,
Visiting the troubled breast
Dost refreshing peace bestow.

Come, O Blessed Spirit of Piety, possess my heart.

God, our Father, may I, through the grace of your Spirit, be forever filled with filial affection for you.

Grant that I may be inspired to love and respect all members of your family as brothers and sisters of Jesus, who, together with him, call you Abba, Father.

Amen.

Pray the Lord's Prayer, the Hail Mary, and the Glory Be.

Fourth Day: The Dignity of the Christian

Thou, in toil art comfort sweet;
Pleasant coolness in the heat;
Solace in the midst of woe.

Come, O Blessed Spirit of Fortitude, uphold my soul in time of trouble and adversity.

O, Divine Trinity, grant that we may be strengthened to see in ourselves and each other the dignity that is ours as temples of Your Holy Spirit, to be loved by one another as each of us is loved by Jesus.

We ask this through Christ, our Lord.

Amen.

Pray the Lord's Prayer, the Hail Mary, and the Glory Be.

Fifth Day: Gifted to Serve and Build Others Up

Light immortal! Light Divine!
Visit Thou these hearts of Thine, And our inmost being fill!

Come, O Blessed Spirit of Knowledge, and grant that I may perceive the will of the Father.

Father, through Your Spirit, You invite us to participate in the fullness of Creation. Help me to see that all gifts are from

Praying with Icons

As beings with five senses, we must use those senses to appreciate things fully. Focusing on icons is an ancient form of prayer that engages our sense of sight. Icons have been part of the Christian tradition for centuries.

An icon is a religious image, usually of Christ, but also of Mary, or the saints painted primarily on wood. Icons are not simply religious art; they are a way into contemplative prayer and are therefore one way to let God speak to us. Icons are carefully painted by an iconographer according to exact and ancient rules about color and design. The piece of wood itself is not sacred; rather the one portrayed in the image (who dwells in heaven) is sacred.

Icons serve as a window into heaven, connecting us with God, as well as a window from heaven to earth, allowing us an intimate connection with God.

The way to pray with an icon is by gazing. As we gaze, the icon begins to speak and to reveal its sacred meaning. Praying with icons is another way to present ourselves to Christ or the saints. It is a tool of prayer, helping us focus on the holy.

Novenas

Nine days—what good could possibly come from a prayer lasting nine whole days?

Well, lots of good!

A novena is a process of praying for nine consecutive periods of time (typically nine days in a row). This planned time of prayer includes periods of reflection on a specific need or petition.

Novenas are based on the nine days Mary and the disciples waited for the coming of the Holy Spirit after Jesus's Ascension, when he was taken up into heaven. On that occasion, Jesus had promised his followers that the Holy Spirit would come upon them so that they could witness to him throughout the world. While they waited for the coming of the Spirit, the Apostles and the women followers of Jesus, including his mother, Mary, devoted themselves to prayer.

Have you ever waited so long for something that it seemed like an eternity? What do you do in the passing of time? Do you wish and hope that things were different and worry about what might come, or do you wait patiently, focus on the present, and trust in God's grace, love, and compassion?

Chapter 6
The Acts and Prayers

Prayers That Express Our Hunger for God

Act of Hope

O my God,
trusting in your infinite goodness and promises, I hope to
obtain pardon for my sins, the
help of your grace, and life
everlasting, through the merits
of Jesus Christ, my Lord and
Redeemer.

Act of Love

O my God,
I love you above all things, with
my whole heart and soul,
because you are all-good and
worthy of all my love. I love
my neighbor as myself for love
of you. I forgive all who have
injured me, and I ask pardon
for all whom I have injured.
Amen.

Act of Contrition

My God, I am sorry for my sins
with all my heart, and I detest
them.
In choosing to do wrong and failing to do good,
I have sinned against you,
whom I should love above all
things.
I firmly intend, with your help,
to do penance, to sin no more,
and to avoid whatever leads me
to sin.
Our savior Jesus Christ suffered
and died for us.
In his name, my God, have
mercy.

Today I Resolve

Lord,
Today I resolve to do the good
You created me to do,
To see the good
You created me to see
To be the good
That you created me to be.
Amen.

The Sacrament of Penance and Reconciliation

Regrettably, the sacrament of Penance and Reconciliation is often misunderstood. This sacrament of healing, forgiveness, and restoration is about much more than telling the priest our sins. The telling isn't the focus of the sacrament; rather, the focus is the forgiveness we receive. The nucleus is not our sins, but is God's mercy! It is about the forgiveness God gives and the grace we receive so we can resolve to "sin no more."

Reconciliation heals our relationship with God and keeps our connection with God strong. When we do something wrong, we often become ashamed and embarrassed. We can find it hard to face God.

Jesus made an interesting remark to Peter when predicting Peter's denial. He said, "But I have prayed for you that your own faith may not fail; and you, when once you have turned back, strengthen your brothers" (Luke 22:32). In other words, Jesus recognized that Peter's guilt might have been so overwhelming that he might have begun to think he could not be forgiven and his faith might fail.

The question isn't whether God will forgive us. The question is whether we have the courage to face ourselves honestly, so we can ask for the forgiveness that God is always ready to give. Don't let your faith fail—turn back to Jesus.

Isaiah 1:18: God's Promise

Come now, let us argue it out,
  says the LORD:
though your sins are like scarlet,
  they shall be like snow;
though they are red like crimson,
  they shall become like wool.

Prayer of Abandonment

Father,
I abandon myself into Your
  hands;
do with me what You will.
Whatever You may do, I thank
  you.

I am ready for all, I accept all.
Let only Your will be done in me
and in all your creatures.
I wish no more than this, O
  Lord.

Into Your hands I commend my
  soul;
I offer it to You
with all the love of my heart,
for I love You, Lord,
and so,
I need to give myself,
to surrender myself,
into Your hands
without reserve
and with boundless confidence,
for you are my Father.
Amen.

                    (Blessed Charles)

Matthew 5:14–16: Be Light

"You are the light of the world. A
city built on a hill cannot be hid.
No one after lighting a lamp puts
it under the bushel basket, but on
the lampstand, and it gives light
to all in the house. In the same
way, let your light shine before
others, so that they may see your
good works and give glory to
your Father in heaven."

Act of Faith

O my God,
I firmly believe you are one
  God in three Divine Persons,
  Father, Son, and Holy Spirit.
I believe in Jesus Christ, your
  Son, who became man and
  died for our sins, and who will
  come to judge the living and
  the dead.
I believe these and all the truth
  which the Holy Catholic
  Church teaches, because you
  have revealed them, who
  can neither deceive nor be
  deceived.
Amen.

The Road Ahead

My Lord God,
I have no idea where I am going.
I do not see the road ahead of
  me.

I cannot know for certain where it will end.
Nor do I really know myself, and the fact that I think I am following your will
does not mean that I am actually doing so.
But I believe that the desire to please you
does in fact please you.
And I hope that I have that desire
in all that I am doing.
I hope that I will never do anything
apart from this desire.
And I know that if I do this, you will lead me by the right road,
though I may know nothing about it.
Therefore I will trust you always, though I may seem to be lost
and in the shadow of death.
I will not fear,
for you are with me
and you will never leave me to face my perils alone.

(Thomas Merton, *Thoughts in Solitude*, p. 83)

Sacred Heart Prayer

Jesus, meek and humble of heart, I ask that I may love you more and more!

O heart of Jesus, burning with love for me,
may my heart burn with love for you.
O Sacred Heart of Jesus, may you be known
and loved throughout the world!
Amen.

Prayer of Serenity

God, grant me the serenity
to accept the things I cannot change,
courage to change the things I can,
and wisdom to know the difference.
Living one day at a time,
enjoying one moment at a time,
accepting hardship as a pathway to peace,
taking, as Jesus did,
this sinful world as it is,
not as I would have it,
trusting that You will make all things right
if I surrender to Your will,
so that I may be reasonably happy in this life
and supremely happy in the next.
Amen.
(Reinhold Niebuhr)

Preparing to Celebrate the Sacrament of Penance and Reconciliation

The more honest a person is with himself or herself, the more meaningful the person will find the sacrament of Penance and Reconciliation to be.

When you began to learn about the sacrament of Penance and Reconciliation, you learned the term *examination of conscience.* Over the years, you may have learned many ways to examine your conscience. Here is a simple reflection that will help you prepare for the sacrament of Penance and Reconciliation. In the following passage from 1 Corinthians 13:4–7, put your name where the word *love* occurs. Honestly facing yourself with this examination will help you see the areas in your life that have not been transformed into love. Then you will able to experience the healing, forgiveness, and restoration the Lord offers in this sacrament.

> Love is patient; love is kind; love is not envious or boastful or arrogant or rude. It does not insist on its own way; it is not irritable or resentful; it does not rejoice in wrongdoing, but rejoices in the truth. It bears all things, believes all things, hopes all things, endures all things.

Saint John Vianney

Saint John Vianney didn't exactly appear to be a man destined for greatness. He found it difficult to be a good student—his classes were hard for him. Though he was a deeply spiritual man, John was labeled as having meager intelligence. He was supposed to go into the military, but just before his regiment was to leave for battle, he went into a church to pray. When he came out, he found his regiment had left without him. John seemed to be a bit of a goof-up. His parents and teachers often had to help him out of one thing or another.

After his ordination into the priesthood, this seemingly insignificant man became a giant. He was assigned to Ars, a town in a remote region of France. He soon became widely known as a priest dedicated to celebrating God's healing in the sacrament of Penance and Reconciliation. By the end of his life, more than twenty thousand people were visiting this man annually as he spent 16 to 18 hours a day celebrating the sacrament of Penance and Reconciliation.

John Vianney is called "The Curé of Ars." The word *curé* is the French term for a parish priest, but its root is the Latin word *curatus*—a word for medical care and healing. Because of his healing touch upon the souls in his care, this gentle giant became a bridge through which people could receive forgiveness and unite more fully with God. Today he is the patron saint of priests—a reminder, perhaps, that no matter what other tasks a priest may have, his most important task is the healing of souls.

Psalm 19:7–14:
Prayer for God's Word

The law of the LORD is perfect,
  reviving the soul;
the decrees of the LORD are sure,
  making wise the simple;
the precepts of the Lord are right,
  rejoicing the heart;
the commandment of the LORD
  is clear,
  enlightening the eyes;
the fear of the LORD is pure,
  enduring forever;
the ordinances of the LORD are
  true and righteous altogether.

More to be desired are they than
    gold,
  even much fine gold;
sweeter also than honey,
  and drippings of the honey-
  comb.

Moreover by them is your servant
    warned;
  in keeping them there is great
  reward.
But who can detect their errors?
  Clear me from hidden faults.
Keep back your servant also from
    the insolent;
  do not let them have dominion
  over me.

Then I shall be blameless,
  and innocent of great
  transgression.

Let the words of my mouth and
    the meditation of my heart
  be acceptable to you,
  O LORD, my rock and my
  redeemer.

Psalm 51:11–15:
Prayer for Renewal

Do not cast me away from your
    presence,
  and do not take your holy
  spirit from me.
Restore to me the joy of your
    salvation,
  and sustain in me a willing
  spirit.

Then I will teach transgressors
  your ways,
  and sinners will return
  to you.
Deliver me from bloodshed,
    O God,
  O God of my salvation,
  and my tongue will sing aloud
  of your deliverance.

O Lord, open my lips,
  and my mouth will declare
  your praise.

Philippians 2:6–11:
Jesus Christ Is Lord!

Though he was in the form of
    God,
    [Jesus] did not regard equality
       with God
    as something to be exploited.
but emptied himself,
    taking the form of a slave,
    being born in human likeness.
And being found in human form,
    he humbled himself,
    and became obedient to the
       point of death—
    even death on a cross.

Therefore God also highly
       exalted him
    and gave him the name
    that is above every name,
so that at the name of Jesus
    every knee should bend,
    in heaven and on earth and
       under the earth,
and every tongue should confess
    that Jesus Christ is Lord,
    to the glory of God the Father.

Chapter 7
Prayers from the Universal Experience

Prayers from Catholic Cultures Throughout the World

Words from Saint Josephine Bakhita of Sudan

I have given everything to my Master: He will take care of me . . . The best thing for us is not what we consider best, but what the Lord wants of us!

I received the Sacrament of Baptism with such joy that only angels could describe . . .

O Lord, if I could fly to my people and tell them of your Goodness at the top of my voice: oh, how many souls would be won!

If I were to meet the slave-traders who kidnapped me and even those who tortured me, I would kneel and kiss their hands, for if that did not happen, I would not be a Christian and Religious today . . .

The Lord has loved me so much: we must love everyone . . . we must be compassionate!

I can truly say that it was a miracle I did not die, because the Lord has destined me for greater things . . .

Mary protected me even before I knew her!

When a person loves another dearly, he desires strongly to be close to the other: therefore, why be afraid to die? Death brings us to God!

Living in Solidarity

The word *namaste* (nah-mah-STAY) is an Asian word, a word commonly used in yoga that means "the divine in me recognizes the divine in you." Imagine what it might be like if, every time you encountered a person, you stopped for a moment to realize that you are created in God's image, and the person in front of you also is made in God's image. What would happen if you thought that when someone was mean to you or gossiped about you? What would happen if you thought that when you were tempted to sin against someone or thought dishonorable things about another person?

Simple words say so much! We are called to be in solidarity with others by recognizing the divine in them. As the word *namaste* implies, we also need to recognize and notice the divine in ourselves. When we are in solidarity, we are able to see the world—a situation, a person, or even a problem—through another person's eyes. Standing in solidarity means standing together, side by side, facing forward, with each person having equal power and equal responsibility.

We can live in solidarity with other people when we include them and their needs in our prayer instead of always asking for something we want for ourselves.

Make Me a Better Christian—El Salvador

God the Father, I give you thanks for all the marvels you have created.

I praise you and I bless you for the inestimable grace of life that you give to us.

Transform me, make me a better Christian, a living testimony of your mercy and of your power.

Strip me, Lord of all roots of bitterness, of false pride and haughtiness of heart.

Make me meek and humble of heart as was our Lord Jesus Christ, and never let me wound with my words or my actions the dignity of any person.

Put in my heart the ardent desire to work earnestly for the poor and the needy.

Show me the garment with which you clothed me the day that I received you as Lord and Savior of my life.

May I wear those garments at the service of my neighbor and of this community.

Use me, Lord, for your work.

(Barbara Ballenger, editor, *Prayer Without Borders,* p. 29)

Prayer to Respect Others—Pakistan

As I walk down dusty roads or busy concrete boulevards, help me, God, to take the time to see in the eyes of the other, to recognize the other, in order to respect.

As I encounter many people, many races, help me to appreciate the hand of the other, to recognize those hands that create and build, in order to work together.

As my path calls me to various places, help me to learn to walk together with others on paths that lead to peace, recognizing that by walking with others, in working together, we learn to recognize ourself in the other, to recognize and appreciate our differences.

And begin to recognize what love is about.

(*Prayer Without Borders,* p. 47)

Prayers from Tanzania

Light a Holy Fire

Receive this holy fire.
Make your lives like this fire.
A holy life that is seen.
A life of God that is seen.
A life that had no end.
A life that darkness does not
overcome.
May this light of God in you
grow.
Light a fire that is worthy of your
heads.
Light a fire that is worthy of your
children.
Light a fire that is worthy of your
fathers.
Light a fire that is worthy of your
mothers.
Light a fire that is worthy of
God.
Now go in peace.
May the Almighty protect you
today and always.
(Desmond Tutu, *An African
Prayer Book,* p. 128)

Father, Thank You

Father, thank you for your revelation and death and illness
and sorrow.
Thank you for speaking so
plainly to us, for calling us all
friends and hovering over us;
for extending your arms out
to us.
We cannot stand on our own;
we fall into death without you.
We fall from faith, left to our
own. We are really friendless
without you.
Your extended arms fill us with
joy, expressing love, love caring
and carrying, asking and receiving our trust.
You have our trust, Father, and
our faith, with our bodies and
all that we are and possess.
We fear nothing when with you,
safe to stretch out and help
others, those troubled in faith,
those troubled in body.
Father, help us to do with our
bodies what we proclaim, that
our faith be known to you and
to others, and be effective in all
the world.
(*An African Prayer Book,*
pp. 65–66)

Diversity and Unity

Jesus sent a significant and resounding message: love the Lord with all your heart and love your neighbor as you love yourself (see Matt. 22:37–39, Mark 12:29–31, Luke 10:27). During his public ministry, Jesus used stories, parables, and miracles to demonstrate to people that all people, of all races, of all languages are God's beloved people. Jesus revealed that God is Father. With God as our Father, we are brothers and sisters who are united in one family.

Despite this unity, we are also unique. We know that God created us each individually with a mind, heart, and soul. We are each created so uniquely different that no other person will ever be or ever has been just like another. This is amazing to think about, knowing that nearly 6.5 billion people live in the world today. Among these billions of people are diverse cultures with their own dress, dance, food, humor, and prayer.

So which is it, diversity or unity? The answer: Yes!

There is a unity of faith. The Bible says, "There is one body and one Spirit, just as you were called to the one hope of your calling, one Lord, one faith, one baptism, one God and Father of all, who is above all and through all and in all" (Eph. 4:4–6). Yet this one faith is expressed in a great diversity of ways. From the clarity of thought from Europe to the attention to nature from tribal cultures, from the festive dance of Africa to the elaborate art of Asia, God's people throughout time and the world have brought beautifully rich expression to the human desire to love the Lord with all your heart and love your neighbor as you love yourself.

Which Way, Lord? What Can I Do?

Patty and Rod were both college-educated adults who had a great deal of concern for others, especially the poor. They felt a desire in their hearts to work for justice. Yet despite all their work for the needy, they felt God was calling them to do more. Because of this sense, they simply asked and found their answer. Against the recommendations and fears of their families, they moved to a poor neighborhood.

To identify *more fully* with the poor, they moved into this neighborhood to live side by side *with* the people there, to be with them and to be one with them. Living in such solidarity allowed Patty and Rod to live closest to what Jesus asks of us—to treat everyone with respect and to love one another.

Thirty-five years later, Patty and Rod are still in the same neighborhood and still work together with their neighbors to develop ways to improve their lives through education, justice awareness, spiritual reflection, and, above all, *recognition of* the dignity and value of every human being.

Interestingly, not only have the people of the neighborhood met Jesus in the faces of Patty and Rod, but Patty and Rod have met Jesus in the faces of their neighbors.

An Irish Blessing

May the road rise up to meet you,
May the wind be always at your back,
May the sun shine warm upon your face,
And the rains fall soft upon your fields,
And until we meet again,
May God hold you in the palm of His hand.

Prayer from the Christian Conference of Asia

Oh God, we take time to pause from daily work to gather our thoughts; to let our souls catch up with our bodies; to feel your presence in our creation; to ask forgiveness for our lapses, ours and on behalf of your people; and to be ourselves restored.

Breathing in, God's Spirit calms my body; breathing out, it's good to be alive.

Lord Jesus Christ, we take time to gather around you. By your life and teachings may we find our strength, and journeying together may we find our rest.

Breathing in, Christ lives in our lives; breathing out, it's good to be alive.

Holy Spirit, creative energy of love and compassion, life embracing, life transforming, heal our bodies, heal our souls, heal our relationships, heal our nations.

Breathing in, the Spirit heals; breathing out, it's good to be alive.

Amen.

(*Prayer Without Borders,* p. 93)

Prayers from Mexico

Praise in the Morning

These are the mornings sung about by David the King!
Today, because it is your saint's day, we sing to you here.

Wake up, my love, wake up!
Look, the day has already dawned.
Already the birds are singing.
The moon has already hidden.
How pretty is the morning today when I come to greet you.

We come all with delight and pleasure to congratulate you!
The day that you were born all the flowers were born.

In the baptismal font sang the nightingales.

The light that God gave is already dawning.

Get up this morning and look: it is already dawn!

From all the stars of heaven I have to bring two:

One to greet you, the other to say to you goodbye.

Today, because it is your saint's day, we desire your happiness.

With clusters of flowers I come to greet you.

And today, because it is your saint's day, we come to sing to you.

(*Prayer Without Borders,* p. 101)

Prayer Before Sleeping

My guardian angel, my sweet company, do not abandon me by night nor by day.

My guardian angel, humbly I ask you, help me and free me from all danger.

Four little angels are in my bed, two at my feet and two at my sides and the Holy Virgin beside me.

She tells me, "O beautiful child, sleep and rest, do not be afraid of anything."

O Blessed Saint Monica, mother of Saint Augustine, bless my little bed, because now I go to sleep.

(*Prayer Without Borders,* p. 49)

The Wayfarer's Prayer

God, you have guided your people throughout their history.

So now as pilgrim children we turn to you, searching for your image and for a place to rest.

Like a good friend, Lord, you are always with the poor.

You make yourself a travel companion to us wayfarers, to us the undocumented, the refugees, the migrants, pilgrims all who walk toward you.

You call us to be witnesses of your love and to be examples of our faith in whatever land receives us.

Lord, may the spirit of Pentecost be renewed.

May all peoples, races and languages be one in communion.

(Youth and Migration Program of the Mexican Commission of Youth Ministry, in *Prayer Without Borders,* p. 51)

Prayer for the Rural and Farming Life—Colombia

Lord Jesus, in images of farming
   and rural life you announced
   your gospel to the poor.
We pray for rural men and
   women, especially for those
   who work hard in the fields.
Give us the strength of your
   Spirit to be witnesses and col-
   laborators of the creative provi-
   dence.
May we always sow in ourselves
   and in our families the holiness and hope of Christian life,
   with the same zeal with which
   we cultivate our land.
Bless the daily efforts of farmers
   and farm workers.
Let all recognize the dignity of
   their labor.
Raise from among us men and
   women at the service of the
   gospel, sisters and brothers to
   announce unceasingly your
   love for this world that is your
   own field and farm.
We give you glory forever and
   ever.
(*Prayer Without Borders,* p. 31)

I Want to Believe, I Will Not Believe—Brazil

I will not believe in the law of
   the strongest, in the language
   of guns, in the power of the
   powerful.
I want to believe in the rights of
   all, in the open hand, in the
   strength of the nonviolent.
I will not believe in race or
   riches, in privileges, in the
   established order.
I want to believe that all human
   beings are human beings and
   that the order of force and of
   injustice is a disorder.
I will not believe that I don't
   have to concern myself with
   what happens far from here.
I want to believe that the whole
   world is my home, the field
   that I sow, and that all reap
   what all have sown.
I will not believe that I can
   combat oppression out there
   if I tolerate injustice here.
I want to believe that what is
   right is the same here and
   there and that I will not be free
   while even one human being is
   excluded.

I will not believe that war and
hunger are inevitable and that
peace is inaccessible.
I want to believe in the love of
bare hands, in peace on earth.
I will not believe that any effort is
in vain. I will not believe that
the dream of human beings
continues being only a dream
and that death is the end.
But I dare to believe in the dream
of God: a new heaven, a new
earth where justice reigns.
(Dom Helder Camara, in *Prayer
Without Borders,* pp. 44–45)

Part III

Methods
for Personal Prayer

Chapter 8
The Lord's Prayer

Praying as Jesus Taught

Praying as a Poem

The following is a poetic break-down of the Lord's Prayer. Several synonyms complement each line. Each synonym portrays or points to a further or deeper meaning of the words of the Lord's Prayer. Make this poem a prayer. Pray it slowly and allow each new word to transform your heart. This poem can bring new life to these familiar words, and the "Lord's Prayer" can have a renewed meaning for you. Add any words that are important to you. This poetic interpretation demonstrates that personal prayer is deep, complex, and substantial—even in the simple words of the Lord's Prayer.

Our: community, together, everyone's, group's, family's, us, we, collectively, jointly, equal, mutual

Father: Creator, origin, destination, mother, parent, maker, Abba, God

who art: exists, lives, breathes, moves, stays, is

in heaven: above, around, in, under, over, everywhere

hallowed be thy name: holy, blessed, special, deep, meaningful, sacred, divine, graceful

thy kingdom come: world, ideal, universe, dream, creation, place, space, home, reign

thy will be done: motivation, strength, desire, hope, reason, trust, witness

on earth: here, with, around, above, below, next to, within, nature

as it is in heaven: the universe, eternity, soul, forever, beyond, over, within

Give us this day: present, now, today, patience, here and now, nearby, current, this moment, for now

our daily bread: nourishment, sustenance, fuel, essentials, needs, necessities

Spontaneous Prayer

A large part of prayer is conversation with God. In prayer, we might ask for something or express gratitude. We might simply tell God how great we believe God is, or we might tell God a problem we are having and simply surrender our problems to God's wisdom.

When we just don't have the words, we can rely on what we already know. Prayers like the Lord's Prayer and Hail Mary can call us to prayer even when we don't know what to say. But we can also speak with God from our hearts, and we can voice our thoughts just as we would to a friend. Such conversation is called spontaneous prayer.

Spontaneous prayer is a great way to talk with God about anything at all. Don't worry about getting caught up in the words to say. Know that God already knows what you need before you ask (see Matt. 6:8). Know that Jesus found himself in times of deep prayer. Many people feel they can't pray. But if we say "God help me. I'm not good at prayer," we have taken the first step to spontaneous prayer! Pray before school. Pray before tests. Pray with a friend in need. Just be in touch with the present moment and invite God to be a part of it. By doing this, you fulfill Saint Paul's command to pray at all times (see 1 Thess. 5:17).

and forgive us our trespasses:
sins, dishonor, disrespect, steal
dignity
as we forgive those: let go,
release, heal, reconcile, renew,
try again, purify
who trespass against us: hurt,
pain, dishonor, mistrust, abandon, abuse, mislead, discredit,
blame, harm
And lead us: guide, teach, show,
allow, gentle, point, coach,
demonstrate, aim, direct, train
not into temptation: lure,
destruction, bitterness, revenge,
injustice
but deliver us: free, arrive, carry,
send, bring, bear, hold, grasp,
endure, support, keep, prevent,
protect, rescue
from evil: wrong, sin, wicked-
ness, immorality, unrest,
trouble, corruption, offense,
attack, malice, hatred
Amen: So be it! Absolutely!
You bet! Yes! I believe it!
Absolutely! Definitely! I agree!

Matthew 6:9–13

"Pray then in this way:
Our Father in heaven,
hallowed be your name.
Your kingdom come.
Your will be done,
on earth as it is in heaven.
Give us this day our daily bread.

And forgive us our debts,
as we also have forgiven our
debtors.
And do not bring us to the time of
trial,
but rescue us from the evil one."

A Format for Personal Prayer

*As you begin to develop your habits
of prayer, trying different styles
and structures of prayer can be
very exciting. The Lord's Prayer
contains seven distinct steps that
can be a structure to a daily prayer
time.*

1. **Our Father in heaven, hallowed be your name.** Often
we pray to God because we are
in need of his help. God is the
awesome Creator of all, the
giver of life and love. Spend
this first part of your prayer
praising God and thanking
God because God is worthy of
all praise and worship.

2. **Your kingdom come.** When
Jesus preached, he preached
Good News. The Good News
is that the Reign of God is
here and it is among us. We
believe this by faith. Our experience, however, tells us that
God's Reign hasn't completely
come. Spend this part of your

prayer asking for God's justice to come. Where are wars? In your community, where are conflicts? How is life, from conception to natural death, threatened? These are some of the things that need prayer.

3. **Your will be done, on earth as it is in heaven.** Before you were born, God knew you. In fact, God knows you better than anyone. God has a vision of the person you can be and of a life of joy and fullness. But rather than seeking the life God has for them, many people resist. During this time of prayer, ask for God's will to be done in you, a will for happiness, joy, and hope.

4. **Give us this day our daily bread.** Because God loves you more than you can imagine, God wants you to bring your needs to him. Are you having trouble with friends? Do you feel the stress of school or family life? Come to the Lord and speak all of your needs. Just by telling God these things, you are making a great act of faith.

5. **And forgive us our debts, as we also have forgiven our debtors.** Scripture is clear

that we can receive forgiveness to the extent that we forgive others. Whom are you mad at? Who has embarrassed you in front of others? Who has betrayed you? The Lord asks you to forgive these people and then to know the fullness of God's forgiveness.

6. **And do not bring us to the time of trial.** Temptation is everywhere we turn—to cheat in school, to lie to our parents, to do things that are against God's will as shown in the Scriptures and in the Church's teaching. We believe, however, that where temptation is, God's help is there even more. Pray for the help you will need when faced with temptations.

7. **But rescue us from the evil one.** The last petition of the Lord's Prayer continues the theme of the struggle between good and evil. It moves from our personal struggle with evil to pray with the whole Church about the distress of the world. Even when we pray in private, we pray in communion with the whole Church for the needs of the whole human family

The Lord's Prayer and the Early Church

Jesus gave the Apostles direct information about how to pray effectively. Jesus gave them (and us!) the words of the Lord's Prayer, or the Our Father.

The Lord's Prayer is considered the perfect prayer because it encompasses all we are called to as Christians. It is the perfect prayer of asking, because it voices our needs, yet acknowledges that we need God's will to be done most of all.

As the early disciples searched for a way to continue the mission that Jesus began, little did they know they would rely on Jesus's prayer instruction after he had left them and returned to heaven.

Pray the Lord's Prayer. Think about how this prayer has helped you in the past. If you cannot think of a time, try to identify how the Lord's Prayer might carry you in the future. Commit yourself to praying the perfect prayer every day.

Saint Teresa of Ávila

Saint Teresa of Ávila was a mystic, a teacher of the art of prayer, a spirit-filled leader of a religious order, a woman of great courage, and an individual who lived life to the fullest. Before that she lost interest in God when she was twelve years old. At age fifteen, her mother died, and Teresa was placed in the care of Augustinian nuns. With these women, her love of God was rekindled.

Throughout her life, Teresa struggled with repeated illnesses, and she struggled with prayer. But in her forties, she was deeply transformed by prayer, in fact, by *the* prayer: the Lord's Prayer.

Sometimes the Lord's Prayer can become such a routine prayer that we don't even listen to the words we are saying. But Teresa found that by joining these words to a mind focused on God, a person could know an intimate, mystical friendship with God. Teresa spoke of prayer as an intimate sharing between friends. Prayer is taking time frequently to be alone with God and having the Lord's Prayer as the basis of the conversation between friends.

Chapter 9
Lectio Divina

Using the Bible in Prayer

The River, the Word

Some people think of the Bible as written in stone, like the stone tablet with the Ten Commandments that Moses carried down the mountain. There is a comfort in thinking of things that don't change. When you pick up your Bible and read it, you are reading ancient words. In the Old Testament, you have the words that God's people, Israel, read. In the entirety of the Scriptures, you hold the same words your parents read, the saints have read, and countless men and women throughout the ages have read. When you turn to the Psalms, you are reading the words Jesus read in his prayer time. In many ways, the thought of the Bible as words written in stone is an accurate one, but not completely accurate.

The words of the Bible also are like a river. A river flows through the land and changes everything around it. If you have ever flown over Las Vegas, you know what water does to a desert. You are flying over brown land . . . brown . . . brown . . . suddenly *green!* The water has changed the desert, making it livable and beautiful.

The word of God flows through your heart, and its ancient truths are meant to change you and the things around you. *Lectio divina,* or "holy reading," is a way of praying with the Scriptures that allows the words you read to flow into every part of you: thoughts, words, and action; body, mind, and soul.

For many of us, reading is a quick process. We usually try to read fast to cover as much as we can in as short a time as possible. But *lectio divina* is slow. It is a relaxed, deliberate reading that is more about depth than breadth.

Sharper Than Any Two-Edged Sword: The Scriptures and the Heart

In the movie *The Flintstones* (1994, 91 minutes, rated PG), Fred, Wilma, Barney, and Betty decide to take a trip to the Grand Canyon. They arrive, and there flowing through the rock is a tiny stream, about 2 inches wide, with a sign posted next to it that says "Grand Canyon." "Yeah," says Barney. "They say this will really be something someday."

If you have ever been to the Grand Canyon, you know that Barney was right. The mighty Colorado River has cut into the rock of that canyon, revealing the beauty in its depths.

If you let it, God's word flowing through your life will change you. It will cut through the things in your life that keep you from being who God has made you to be. Sometimes those things the river needs to cut through are sin and wrongdoing. Other times it has to cut through the limits you put on yourself. Have you ever said to yourself, "I could never . . ." Well, maybe you could. If you let God's word cut through, it will show you that your heart is as amazing as the Grand Canyon, as powerful, as beautiful.

Lectio divina begins with developing the ability to listen deeply and to hear with the ear of your heart. *Lectio divina* requires patience with yourself as you learn to slow down. You learn to quiet down. You learn the rhythm of this form of prayer. *Lectio divina* requires courage, because silence can feel uncomfortable. We live in a noisy world. We get in our cars and turn on the radio. We walk in our homes and turn on the television. The silence of *lectio divina* invites us to push past the discomfort of psychological silence and find the refreshment of spiritual silence.

The question in your heart during *lectio divina* is not "Is God speaking to me?" but rather "What is God saying to me?" In *lectio divina,* you move into the recesses of your heart where God dwells.

The Four R's of *Lectio Divina*

Introduction

As you begin learning *lectio divina,* you may find it helpful to use the Psalms for your reading.

Perhaps you start at the beginning and read a new section each day. Perhaps you use the Psalms for the Mass readings of the day. Remember, *lectio divina* is about depth, not breadth. The passage you choose ought not be too long. Although the form of *lectio divina* is not rigid or set in stone, it does have a four-part process, the four R's: reading *(lectio),* reflecting *(meditatio),* responding *(oratio),* and resting *(contemplatio).*

Reading *(Lectio)*

Begin reading with your heart and mind focused on the God who dwells in the very word you read. Draw near to the word with the same reverence with which you approach the Blessed Sacrament at church. With this reverence, read.

And read again . . . and read again . . . and again. You are listening for words or phrases that resonate within your heart. Read your words and phrases aloud. Read what attracts your heart.

Reflecting *(Meditatio)*

In reflecting, ponder the words you have read. Imitate Mary, who "treasured all these words and pondered them in her heart" (Luke 2:19). God's word is alive with power and meaning. In this step of *lectio divina,* ask yourself, "What does this mean?" or "What does this mean to me?" Let the life of the word give you life as you consider how the ancient words you read speak to you today.

The temptation of the reflecting step of *lectio divina* is to make it an intellectual exercise. Remember, the primary activity of reflecting is listening. In reflecting, look for God's light shining on the words before you. In this holy light, see in new ways, hear with new ears. In reflecting, "let the word of Christ dwell in you richly" (Col. 3:16).

Responding *(Oratio)*

You might think of prayer as conversation with God. In the first step, reading, God has spoken to you. In the second step, reflecting, you spend time understanding God's message. In responding, it is your turn. Let your heart speak to God. As you understand the passage, what does it make you want to pray for? Do you want to thank God, praise God, ask God's forgiveness, complain to God, ask for God's help, or pray for others?

Prayer is the cry of your heart. Prayer is tears. Prayer is joy. Prayer is asking. Prayer is offering. Prayer is the gift you give to God.

The Bible as God's Word

You are sitting in Mass, listening to the first reading, the responsorial psalm, the second reading, then, with an "Alleluia!" the congregation stands to greet the Gospel.

Reading the Bible as God's word means that even if you are sitting on your bed or in your favorite chair, your heart is standing, attentive, because God's word is different from all other words. God's word is alive, and it gives life to everything around it—including you.

When we go to Mass, we believe Jesus is truly present in the Eucharist. He also is present in the priest and in the praying and singing of the people. He is also present in the word. Of these four ways that Jesus is present at Mass, the Scriptures are the only one you can have with you in your room. Do you want Jesus to be present? Read the word.

God is speaking to you as you read the word. What is God saying? Let your heart be standing and attentive.

Saint Jerome

The next time you pick up your Bible, think of Saint Jerome. He was a priest and scholar who lived in the fourth century AD.

The Pope commissioned Jerome to revise the translation of the Bible. As Catholics we have had a glimpse of some of the struggles Jerome faced when he revised the Bible, because in recent years, the translation we use at Mass has also gone through revisions. Some people do not think the changes are good; others welcome them, believing that the changes make the words more meaningful, perhaps more accurate to their original version.

Jerome had both fans and critics, and the discussions weren't always pleasant. But this scholar loved the word of God and wanted to make it understood. While some focused on an exact, word-for-word translation of the Bible, Jerome focused on translating the overall meaning.

Jerome raised a great question: "How do you and I make the word of God understood by the people we meet each day?" As people who believe in God's word, we are asked to live God's word in a way that makes God known to those we meet.

Resting *(Contemplatio)*

Too many times, we are tempted to end our prayer after we have talked, but there is yet another step: resting in the presence of God.

Have you ever been on a long drive with a friend in which the two of you said little? Consider such silence between two friends—the comfort, the solace, the joy of knowing that you are understood, that you are loved. In resting, you realize you have connected with the Spirit of God, and you wait there, you let your heart dwell there, you stay and let God love you.

Perhaps you are concerned: "Will I be able to hear God?" Yes. Remember, your heart was made to find its way to God.

"Likewise the Spirit helps us in our weakness; for we do not know how to pray as we ought, but that very Spirit intercedes with sighs too deep for words" (Rom. 8:26). The Spirit prays for us when we have no words of our own and listens for us when we find it hard to hear the words of God. Yes, your heart will find its way to God.

In *lectio divina,* our souls absorb the word of God. Then it flows from us into the world, giving life and changing everything around us.

The Four R's of *Lectio Divina*

1. Reading *(Lectio)*

Take your time and read the passage. Get a sense of what it is saying. Read the passage a second time. Pause on any words or phrases that strike you, and listen in your heart.

2. Reflecting *(Meditatio)*

As you pause on the words or phrases that strike you, ask yourself the following questions:

- What does this passage mean?
- What does this passage mean to me or for my situation?

3. Responding *(Oratio)*

As you get a sense of the passage's meaning, ask yourself the following questions:

- What does this passage want me to pray for?
- What does this passage make me want to say to God?

4. Resting *(Contemplatio)*

Take time to be attentive to your heart, where God moves, lives, and speaks within you. Ask yourself the following question:

- What do I feel God is saying back to me now that I have responded to God?

Chapter 10
Guided Meditation

Entering the Stories of Jesus

Every moment is alive with God. Every moment, past, present, and future, is full of God's presence and power. Learning to be fully alive to the moment today means you are prepared for the tomorrows to come.

Guided meditation is a prayer form that relies heavily on the imagination. It is also a form of prayer that relies heavily on the senses. Guided meditation awakens you to your surroundings, relationships, feelings, and thoughts. It guides you in prayer to an encounter or an exchange with Jesus, and it helps you become more aware of God's presence in the world after prayer.

Scriptural Meditation

In a guided meditation with a Bible passage, the Scriptures become alive to you. You place yourself into the scriptural account and become a character in the story: a disciple, a bystander, one being healed, or even Jesus.

Getting Started

To begin guided scriptural meditation, choose a Scripture passage. The following may provide some good places to look:

- the Gospel for the day's Eucharistic liturgy (The daily readings from the liturgy can be found at the Web site for the United States Conference of Catholic Bishops.)
- the reading from the upcoming Sunday's Eucharistic liturgy
- a Bible passage someone has given you that means a lot to you
- a passage that was used on a retreat or other event you attended

Can We Hear God's Voice in Prayer?

Yes, we can hear God's voice in prayer! But are we listening?

God's manner of speaking to God's people is as unique as the people themselves. Each of us hears God in our own way, because God speaks to us in a way that we can hear him.

We hear most voices with our ears. God speaks to us through our hearts, through our eyes, and in our souls. God's voice is an impression, a knowing that calls us toward something.

A common obstacle to hearing God is simply this: we often dismiss the ways in which God speaks. A thought goes through our mind that we dismiss as silly. A comment someone makes hits us for a moment, but instead of pausing to reflect or write it down, we go about our day. We see a connection between a Scripture passage we are reading and a situation a friend is facing, but we don't tell the friend because we are afraid the friend will think it is dumb. Listen and act!

Once you have selected the passage, take a few moments to call to mind that you are in the presence of God. Turn off radios, phones, and pagers and just sit comfortably.

Imagine that the air you breathe is the Holy Spirit As you breathe in, you breathe in the Holy Spirit. As you breathe out, you release the noise in your mind or soul.

Continue until you experience calm and peace.

Entering into the Reading

Pick up your Bible and read the passage. Read it more than once, but during this first reading, simply become familiar with the passage.

Read the passage again. This time choose a person in the passage and imagine you are experiencing the story as that person—a disciple, a bystander, someone Jesus is interacting with, or Jesus himself. Use your imaginary senses to pay close attention to the surroundings. Ask yourself the following questions:

- What do I see?
- What do I feel?
- What do I smell?
- What do I hear?

- If the story involves food and drink, what do I taste?

Reacting to the Story

Read the passage again. Pay close attention to your feelings and to the reaction of others in the story.

- How do others react to the situation?
- What do I feel through the action in the story?
- What are my thoughts as this action takes place?

Praying Through the Story

Now that you have fully entered into the story with your senses, mind, and feelings, it is time to interact with Jesus beyond the bounds of the story. As you are aware of yourself as a character, what do you want to pray for here and now? Do want to be a better disciple? Do you need to experience Jesus's forgiveness for something you have done? Are you brokenhearted and in need of Jesus's healing? Do you need to heal others as Jesus did? Take time to voice your thoughts and feelings to Jesus and allow him to change you.

Imaginative Prayer Through an Event

The Scriptures offer a ready-made place for you to enter into a story of Jesus. Other events can offer this as well, especially the sacraments. Although you may not have a memory of your Baptism, you can experience it through your imagination. Ideally, another person would read the following meditation as your imagination guides you through the events. You could certainly lead others through the meditation if you are asked to lead prayer at your church, school, or elsewhere.

This meditation on Baptism can also be used when you are alone. Read it slowly, pray through the following event, and allow yourself to be guided—by Jesus. As it feels natural to you, stop and paint the scene with your mind's eye. Pay attention to your feelings and speak to Jesus from your heart.

Meditation on Your Baptism

You are sitting barefoot at the grassy edge of a river. The weather is beautiful, and it is very peaceful here. You close your eyes, and you feel the heat of the yellow sun on your face. You hear the splashing of the current as the water quickly moves downstream.

A noise close by startles you. You sit up and see a quiet, patient-looking man standing not too far from you. You recognize the beard and eyes, and you realize the man is Jesus. He smiles as he approaches and sits down next to you. He greets you by name. Hear yourself respond to him. Notice how you feel to be with Jesus. Hear him tell you that he is happy to have this time alone with you and that there are things he wants to discuss with you. You watch Jesus as he turns his eyes to look at the river. He tells you the water reminds him of his cousin John, who baptized him in the Jordan River. There is affection on his face and in his voice as he speaks of John.

Distractions in Prayer

"My mind wanders!" "What's wrong with me? Why can't
I stay focused in prayer?" These are often-heard comments
when it comes to prayer. We view these mental wanderings
as evidence that we are failing at prayer.

What if these mental wanderings are not an obstacle to
prayer but, in fact, can be a guide to prayer?

If you are praying and you find your mind has wandered,
pause and note what has come to your mind. Perhaps your
mind has turned to a particular decision you need to make.
Maybe a friend you are worried about comes to mind.

Instead of dismissing the situation from your mind, look
for a connection between the Scripture passage and the "dis-
traction." For example, if you find yourself thinking about a
friend whom you are worried about, there may be something
in that Scripture passage that will help your friend.

You can connect the place to which your mind has wandered to the place where you started—namely, your prayer.

Father Walter Burghardt

Hundreds of years from now, Catholics may look at today's time period in the Church and regard Fr. Walter Burghardt as a priest who helped a generation of Catholics learn how to live the Gospel of Jesus Christ.

Burghardt is one of today's most influential preachers. He has urged his hearers to use their belief to make a difference in how they live and in how they relate to the world around them, particularly to those who are less fortunate.

In his writings and homilies, Burghardt enters the Scriptures through guided meditation and experiences them as fully alive. He looks not only at the main character of the story but also at the people and the culture around the story. He then draws on his experience and turns his attention toward today's questions.

Through his fully alive reflection on the Scriptures, Burghardt invites us to consider what these stories mean for us as individuals and for the Church today.

Listen as Jesus talks with you about his baptism and where it took him. Hear Jesus share with you some of the highlights of his life.

Now Jesus looks into your eyes. Hear him ask you to renew your baptismal commitment. Trust him as he reminds you that he will be there to help you always. Together you discuss what truly living out your Baptism means. You talk about what areas in your life need changing or improving. Perhaps you talk about relationships . . . or things you've done that you are not proud of . . . or things you haven't done that you could do. . . . Just share with Jesus everything that keeps you from really living your life as a committed Christian.

Jesus now asks you what good things you have done lately and asks you to share the times when you have really followed him.

Listen as Jesus thanks you for your goodness. Hear him tell you how much good you can accomplish in his name. Notice your feelings as Jesus tells you this.

Jesus stands up and bends forward to offer you a hand. He pulls you up to stand beside him. Notice your reaction when

Jesus invites you into the water to be renewed. Follow Jesus. As you come closer to the river, you begin to feel the rocky sand under your feet. You smile at each other as you feel the first sensation of the cold water swirling around your lower legs. You wade in as far as your knees and stop. Cupping both of his palms together, Jesus bends and dips his hands into the water. His eyes sparkle as he pours the cool water over your head. He prays for you. Listen as he prays.

There is a stillness once Jesus has finished his prayer. Jesus does not move but, instead, seems to be waiting for something. His head remains bowed. Then a powerful but gentle voice fills the air. The voice speaks directly to you and seems to surround you on all sides as it proclaims, "This is my beloved child in whom I am well pleased." Allow yourself to remain quiet and take this in. Know that it has been said to you, about you.

(Adapted from Jane E. Arsenault and Jean R. Cedor, leaders guide for *Guided Meditations for Youth on Sacramental Life,* pp. 11–17).

Reflecting on the Meditation

Take some time to reflect on the following questions for the experience to become a part of you:

- How did I feel when Jesus asked me to renew my baptismal commitment?
- What areas of my life did I share with Jesus that need changing or improving if I am to live as a committed Christian?
- When have I faithfully followed Jesus? What good things have I done? What did Jesus say to me after I had shared the good things I have done?
- What were my feelings as Jesus pulled me up and led me into the river?
- What did Jesus say in his prayer for me as he poured the water over my head?
- How did I feel when I heard the voice proclaim, "This is my beloved child in whom I am well pleased"?

Chapter 11
Journaling

Discovering Ourselves, Discovering the Lord

Journaling is a spiritual practice that is both self-revealing and God-revealing.

For those who are committed to growing in prayer, in relationship with God, and in understanding of how God works in their life, journaling can be a critical piece. Once pen touches paper, it is amazing what things flow out.

In addition to building your spiritual life, journaling helps empty you of the present day and start tomorrow with a clean slate. In your journal, you can pour your heart out to God, who always hears and receives you.

A journal can help you stay thankful to God. Isn't it easy to forget about the prayers God has answered? By writing your prayers in your journal—both petitions

and thanks—you remain ever grateful to God, because your journal reminds you of what God has done.

Journaling takes a bit of practice to do well. Certainly, those who are writers by nature adopt the practice more quickly, but anyone can learn to journal in a way that is both helpful and meaningful. To develop any good habit, you must do the same thing repeatedly until you do it instinctively. For example, let's say that for the last month, you have taken 5 minutes to journal before going to bed. One night you are in bed and you feel as though you have forgotten something. Your journal! You know you have a good habit if you miss it when it is gone.

Personal Salvation History

In the Old Testament Book of Deuteronomy, you often see the word *remember*. The Hebrew people living in the Promised Land were urged to continually remember the good things God had done for them.

In the same way, you need to look at the past to see how God guided and still guides your personal history. This history is the story of your life in God, your salvation!

One method for exploring your salvation history is to brainstorm a list of the most important events of your life—from your earliest memories to your most recent significant moments. What is an important event? You be the judge. It might be an accident, an award, a meeting with a friend, a crisis in your family, an accomplishment, a revealing conversation. Be as thorough as possible in making your list.

In your desire to be closer to God, it can be tempting to think you need a "religious experience" to know God's love for you. These experiences happen for some on retreats or at the Eucharist. For many, such overwhelming experiences do not happen. Rather, God's love is seen over time. After finishing your list, read it over slowly. How has God shown love for you over time? This is your personal salvation history. (Adapted from Carl Koch, *PrayerWays,* p. 94)

Getting Started

Decide on a Journal

As you begin your practice of journaling, choose a journal that is comfortable for you to write in. For example, people often prefer a spiral binding with a hard back. You will also want to decide where you will keep your journal. It is important to treat your journal respectfully; it will carry things from the deepest part of you.

Choose the Right Time of Day

The next step is deciding when you will journal. This takes a bit of practice to see what works best for you. Some prefer the morning, when they can pour out their hopes for the day. Others prefer the evening, when journaling becomes an examining and emptying exercise. Perhaps you will find that a bit of both works for you.

How you use your journaling time also requires some work to see what works best for you. If journaling is new for you, you may find one of the following formats a helpful way to begin.

Journaling in the Morning

At the conclusion of your morning prayer, take a moment and write in your journal the impressions you had from your prayer, ways you felt God might be speaking, or things you think God may be asking you to do. Finally, write a prayer of offering, giving God your heart and your day.

Journaling in the Evening

Write a list of those things you remember from your day, the moments that seemed significant, even if you don't know why. If you recorded a morning journal entry, read your entry to see if those moments from your day connect with anything from your morning prayer. Write about the connections you see. Finally, write a prayer to God, letting go of your day by placing it in God's hands. Ask God to use your sleep to heal you and draw you closer to God.

Try Different Techniques

You can use several techniques in journaling. Similar to finding the right time to write, finding the technique that works best for you and your style is helpful. Look over these different styles and experiment with them. You may find that a particular style works well, but not all the time. Refer to these styles often. You may find that the technique depends on your mood.

Free Writing

Free writing means exactly that—writing freely and sponta-neously whatever comes to mind, letting ideas and feelings flow out unchecked. When free writing, try to write continuously, hardly lifting pen from paper. If you get stuck, write a word or phrase over and over until something else comes to mind.

Try to take a playful attitude toward this sort of journal writ-ing. Chances are, you will uncover some surprises, and that is the point of free writing. After free writing, you may decide to exam-ine one of the surprises further, using another journal-writing technique.

Composing Unsent Letters

If you have ever been furious with someone but knew you could not tell the person of your anger directly, or if you have ever fallen madly in love but were afraid to express your feelings out loud, then you probably can understand the value of writing a letter that will not be sent. Sometimes just the exercise of writing can help get rid of your anger or name your love.

Writing unsent letters in your journal gives you a chance to say anything to anyone, especially to God. Also, writing unsent letters gives you a sense of having an audience with whom to commu-nicate. Many of us find writing to a person easier than just writ-ing on a blank sheet of paper.

Writing Dialogue

Even when you do free writing, a dialogue is going on inside you. You respond to some question buzzing around in your mind. The question might be "What was I thinking about when I did that?" or "How do I really feel about this?" In any case, most writing reacts to a question or a series of internal statements.

Feelings in Prayer

The feelings you experience during prayer can be an entry-way into deeper prayer. Think of it this way: when something happens, your first reaction isn't verbal; rather, it is in your gut—your feelings.

How do you think you would feel if you found out a friend talked about you behind your back? You might *feel* the hurt before you *talked about* the hurt. What do your feelings reveal about you? They reveal that you love your friend. They show that you know betrayal is not part of a good friendship.

Prayer requires everything of you: thoughts, body, soul, and feelings. Your feelings in prayer can help you realize things that are not at the surface.

Some people are surprised to experience loneliness during prayer. Isn't this the opposite of the feeling you should have? Why is loneliness present? If you examine yourself, you might find that the loneliness reveals that you have an ability to follow God even when it is difficult.

What feelings do you have in prayer? What do they reveal about you and what you believe? Take a moment with your journal and reflect on your feelings. You might understand yourself and God in a deeper way.

Saint Thérèse, the Little Flower

Saint Thérèse of Lisieux, the Little Flower, is among the most beloved of saints. She lived only a short time, yet her life gave testimony to the power of love. This testimony of God's love has been given to the world through her journal, *The Story of a Soul.*

Thérèse faced sorrow as a little girl when her mother died. Her family gathered around to help support her in her grief. Her father, "Papa," went with Thérèse on walks to a church where they prayed before the Eucharist every evening after school. Their walks and prayers together helped each heart heal as they grieved the loss of mother and wife.

At age nine, Thérèse experienced another loss. Her sister Pauline, her "second mother," left to join a convent. Thérèse felt shocked and abandoned, but before long, she said that she too would join the convent and did so at the age of fifteen.

Thérèse's spiritual life began to take her to something she called "the little way": loving God in the smallest of things. Through her journal, she realized powerful insights and new understandings of God. Today, hundreds of years after Thérèse's death, thousands of people have read her little way.

Sometimes, stating the questions explicitly and then answering them can help you understand what you are thinking about and feeling. When you write both the questions and your answers, you engage in a dialogue. All sorts of insights can result. You begin to see two sides of an issue. You take the part of someone else and view the matter at hand from her or his point of view. In short, you gain various perspectives. Helpful dialogue partners might be other people, the Father, Jesus, the Holy Spirit, your body, or your emotions.

Using a Prayer Journal

Many people write daily prayers to God as a way of keeping company with God. You can include numerous types of prayers in your journal: you can ask God for help or strength, express sorrow to the Lord about something, reflect on scriptural passages, give thanks and praise, and so on. However, a prayer journal does not have to be limited to forms of prayer such as these. Prayers can be any expression of what you want to say to God.

Seek God's Help

Finally, before you begin writing, ask the Holy Spirit to use your journal to open your heart, eyes, and ears to the work of God in your life.

By continuing this particular journaling practice, you will begin to see ways that God works in your life. You will grow in understanding of how to listen. You will learn to recognize the events in your life that seem ordinary but are actually openings through which God is reaching out to you.

(This chapter is adapted from Carl Koch, *PrayerWays,* pp. 91–93.)

Part IV

Liturgical Prayer

Chapter 12
Liturgical Prayer

The Body of Christ:
Past, Present, and Future

Family History

What do you know about your family history? Did your grandmother or grandfather ever show you photographs of their grandparents? As you looked at the pictures, did you realize you resemble these people who share your DNA but who died long before you were born?

What do you know about your spiritual history? In the same way that your body shares DNA with your relatives, past and present, you also share a sort of spiritual DNA with people beyond your physical family. These people are your brothers and sisters, past and present, in Jesus Christ.

Gathering with the Church Present

When you gather with others for liturgical prayer—the Eucharist, the Liturgy of the Hours, the sacrament of Penance and Reconciliation, the Anointing of the Sick, and so forth—you gather with the people in your parish. But liturgical prayer is about gathering with so many more than those you see. You are gathering with Catholics in Kenya, Ireland, and Mexico. You are gathering with Catholics in Poland, Brazil, and Tanzania. Wherever the liturgy is celebrated, it is fundamentally the same. For example, did you know that no matter where in the world you go to Mass on a given Sunday, you would hear the same readings being read in your own parish? Well, you would, assuming you understood the language!

Gathering with the Church Past

Pick up an apple. A long time ago, someone planted apple seeds in an orchard. From one of those trees came hundreds of apples. The apple grower sold his apples, and now people all over your area eat apples that came from the same tree as yours did. Imagine that you planted the seeds of your apple, grew an apple tree, and gave away your apples. Through your planting and giving, the circle that the original tree started has grown. And imagine that those people planted seeds and sold apples, and then those people did. Over the course of time, thousands of people would eat apples that came from the same tree.

In this analogy, the Last Supper is the apple tree. This is when Jesus "took a loaf of bread, and when he had given thanks, he broke it and gave it to them, saying, 'This is my body, which is given for you. Do this in remembrance of me'" (Luke 22:19). Something about that moment burned upon the hearts of the disciples.

The disciples continued this meal as Jesus commanded—"in remembrance." They went forth and began to evangelize and break bread with women and men who came to believe in Jesus. And for the past two thousand years, we have been receiving from the same tree.

When we gather at Mass, we gather with the disciples and with all those who have gone before us. We sit at the table of the Last Supper, and we "take" and "eat" (see Matthew 26:26). In this way, the Last Supper is never truly past but is always present, always among us.

Gathering to Become the Body of Christ

At every moment in the day, the Eucharistic liturgy is celebrated somewhere in the world. This celebration makes the past alive—the Last Supper is alive. At any celebration of the Eucharist, those who gather are transported in time and space. In the middle of a seemingly ordinary homily, in the middle of a ritual they have heard over and over again, in the middle of songs that may or may not be on key, all people are brought into the presence of the risen Lord Jesus. He is real and he is there.

You gather with your present needs in your heart. At the Eucharist, you receive an invitation to bring your life, joys, pains, laughter, and sorrow and to join them to Jesus. You place yourself into the bread and into the cup. Within the bread and cup, you find your brothers and sisters who have also placed themselves in the bread and cup, and you are united right then, in that moment.

The Eucharist is all about communion. You gather with your brothers and sisters all over the world. You gather with your sisters and brothers who gathered two thousand years ago. You gather to be in communion with God.

Communion, or "with union," is an interesting word for us Catholics. It describes the unity among us. It describes our relationship with God, and it describes the consecrated bread and wine that we receive when we come forward at the Eucharist.

But here is the mind-blowing thing: Catholics believe that the Communion we receive enables us to become the communion that we are called to—with God and with one another. In other words, the Body of Christ we hold in our hands gives us the grace to become the Body of Christ that is the Church, the home of God.

The Eucharistic Liturgy: The Body of Christ Receives the Body of Christ to Become the Body of Christ

When we Catholics are called to the Eucharistic liturgy, we are called to participate with our hearts, minds, and bodies, or as the Church says, we are called to full, conscious, and active participation.

"But I don't get anything out of Mass!" This is a common regret many people, particularly young people, express. The Church calls us to extreme participation, but how can we fulfill that vision the Church holds?

Come Early

Being early to a party can make many people feel self-conscious. At times like those, the early arrivals and the host may glance out the window, hoping someone else comes in, someone fun, someone familiar. There is usually the person who arrives fashionably late. Everyone is there, beginning to warm up to one another, when the life of the party shows up, and everyone else relaxes.

No doubt, the Eucharist is a celebration, but it is not a party. Come, and come early.

Take the moments before Mass to present yourself before God. Allow yourself time to pray and ask for God's will to be done in your life. Look at the altar and think about the great event that will happen in half an hour or so. Simply be at peace in God's presence.

Sometimes it is good to use your own words—no one knows your own heart better than you and God. Your words flow from your heart to God's.

Sometimes it is good to use other people's words, such as the prayers found in this book. In this way, you begin to experience the ancient nature of the Catholic faith. As you pray, think about the thousands of Catholics who have used the same words to lift their hearts to God.

In October 1962, Pope John XXIII gathered the leaders of the Church—cardinals, bishops, theologians, and philosophers—in Rome for the Second Vatican Council, saying that the Church needed a fresh approach to its timeless teachings.

When the council concluded in 1965, the council members defined that fresh approach for the Church and its members. In one of the writings from the council, a fresh approach was provided for the Eucharist.

Consider this excerpt from that writing:

> But in order that the Liturgy may be able to produce its full effects, it is necessary that the faithful come to it with proper dispositions, that their minds should be attuned to their voices, and that they should cooperate with divine grace lest they receive it in vain.[1] ("Constitution on the Sacred Liturgy *Sacrosanctum Concilium,*" no. 11)

Proper Disposition

Though the term can sound vaguely scolding, having the *proper disposition* is pretty much key to learning anything. Have you ever been in a class with a know-it-all, someone who had an answer for everything? That person, no matter what the topic, always had "the exact same thing" happen to him or her. Annoying, isn't it? How much do you think that person is learning?

Having a proper disposition when you come to Mass simply means that you present yourself to God with an open heart. Rather than assuming the disposition of a know-it-all, you assume the disposition of a disciple. Your heart is focused on the God who calls you to come to the Eucharist, to communion with God and the Church. With your open heart focused on God, you are in a position to hear and respond to God.

Before going to church, here are some practical things you can do at home to help place you in the proper disposition:

- **Read the Scripture readings.**
  Refer to chapter 9 of this book
  and use the *lectio divina* method of prayer with a Gospel or
  one of the other readings.
- **Look outside yourself.** Ask
  yourself two simple questions
  before you go to the Eucharist:
  Where has it been easy to see
  or feel the Lord during the past
  week? Where has it been hard
  to see or feel the Lord during
  the past week? The answers to
  such questions can open your
  heart to hearing God's voice at
  the liturgy.
- **Look inside yourself.**
  Consider your thoughts,
  words, and actions, the things
  you have done and the things
  you have failed to do. How
  have you been Christlike
  through the week? Give thanks
  for the ways you have been
  Christlike. Seek Jesus's help to
  be more like him in the ways
  that you haven't.
- **Look around yourself.**
  Consider the people you know
  and love. How do they need
  God's presence in their lives?
  Is someone sick? Is someone
  moving? Is someone wor-
  ried and anxious? Bring those
  people within your heart to the
  Eucharist.

Minds Attuned to Voices

Have you ever been to Mass, lis-
tened to the Gospel reading, sat
down to listen to the homily, and
realized you can't remember what
the Gospel reading was?

Your voice says amazing things
during the Mass. Are you listening to what you are saying?
"I believe in one God,
  the Father almighty,
  maker of heaven and earth,
  of all things visible and invisible."
"For the kingdom,
  the power and the glory are yours
  now and for ever."
"Lamb of God, you take
  away the sins of the world,
  have mercy on us."
(Roman Missal)

If your mind is attuned to
your voice, the words take on
meaning. The prayers of the
Mass become rich with meaning. At the sign of peace, you
truly extend the peace of Christ
when you greet the person next
to you, rather than extending a
weak "hi how are ya" handshake.

During the Eucharist, you can
fully, consciously, and actively
participate. You can pray the
words of the liturgy in the following ways:

God . . . All in All

What does the Church ask of you at the Eucharist? How does God meet you at Mass? How are you called to participate? Consider the following words from the Church:

> The Church, therefore, earnestly desires that Christ's faithful, when present at this mystery of faith, should not be there as strangers or silent spectators; on the contrary, through a good understanding of the rites and prayers they should take part in the sacred action conscious of what they are doing, with devotion and full collaboration. They should be instructed by God's word and be nourished at the table of the Lord's body; they should give thanks to God; by offering the Immaculate Victim, not only through the hands of the priest, but also with him, they should learn also to offer themselves; through Christ the Mediator,[2] they should be drawn day by day into ever more perfect union with God and with each other, so that finally God may be all in all. ("Constitution on the Sacred Liturgy," no. 48)

Saint Augustine of Hippo

Saint Augustine was born AD 354. You have probably heard many stories like his.

Augustine was raised by a Christian mother, who taught him about matters of faith. He went to a religious school and was a pretty good student. His father hoped to get enough money together to send Augustine to higher education, but it took awhile. During that time, Augustine got into all kinds of stuff. He was into the social scene big time. He got caught up in strange religions. He fathered a son with a woman who was not his wife. Augustine lived for nothing more than his personal enjoyment.

But then something happened. Through his mother's intervention and that of a bishop named Ambrose, Augustine returned to the faith of his childhood. He again embraced Christianity. Eventually he became a bishop and one of the greatest Christian thinkers.

Augustine loved words and philosophy. One of the phrases he made popular was *totus Christus*—the whole Christ. He saw that at the Eucharist, the whole Christ was made present and was unified. He defined the whole Christ as Jesus himself *and* all Christians. We are members of Christ himself. At the Eucharist, this becomes a reality. At the Eucharist, Christians are united to Jesus and to one another, making one body and one spirit, receiving love from the Father and giving love back to the Father.

- **Absorb the environment.**
  God comes to you through your senses. You see and hear God's word. You feel the embrace of God's love through friends and family. You smell Easter in the lilies. You touch your Baptism in the holy water. You are called to change your life in the purple of Lent. Engage your senses upon entering the Church and absorb the message of the Gospel.

- **At the gathering song, gather!**
  The opening song is intended to unite into one voice those who have gathered. Sing out. Listen to those around you. Praise God and begin to unify yourself with the people with whom you will soon commune.

- **Pay attention to the preparation of the gifts.** Sadly, the presentation of the bread and wine is often overshadowed by the collection of money. A good symbol is found in offering your money during that time, but don't stop there. Put yourself in the bread and cup. Because you have prepared yourself, you have something to offer. Join your hopes, work, prayers, concerns, hurts, worries, and every other part of yourself to the bread and cup. As these are changed into the body and blood of Christ, your life, too, can be changed into the body and blood of Christ.

- **Make peace.** Sometimes when you go to the Eucharist, you may sit next to people, either family or friends, who have offended you or whom you have offended. The sign of peace before Communion is a time to make real peace with those people. Say "I'm sorry" or "I love you."

- **Receive in joy.** The greatest moment of unity in the liturgy is when everyone receives the body and blood of Christ. What a joyful moment! Take the sacred body and precious blood and know that you are in communion with the Body of Christ—Jesus himself and all members of his body.

Cooperate with Grace

The writings of the Second Vatican Council tell us that it is through the liturgy, especially the Eucharist, that "the work of our redemption is accomplished" ("Constitution on the Sacred Liturgy," no. 2).

Much of Catholic life involves the visible and the invisible. The visible is both the means through which we receive grace and a reminder of the grace that God gives. The visible of the Mass is the Eucharist—the bread, which has become the body of Christ, and the wine, which has become the blood of Christ. The invisible is the grace that flows from the body and blood of Jesus Christ.

Through presenting yourself at Mass with a proper disposition, with your mind attuned to your voice, grace pours into your heart. Your soul becomes engaged by the power and love of God it receives. Your soul begins to respond; you feel a stirring toward something. The stirring shows itself in quiet ways. This stirring is given so that you may be the living presence of Jesus in the world and that you may continue to be changed into his body and blood. At the end of the liturgy, you are dismissed, sent to change and be changed. For example:

- **The sacrament of Penance and Reconciliation.** Cooperating with divine grace means you go to Penance and Reconciliation. The work of being Christlike involves being honest, painfully honest. Where do you offend God? How do you hurt others? When are you untrue to yourself? In Penance and Reconciliation, you are brought into harmony and your sins are forgiven.

- **Be light.** "The light shines in the darkness" (John 1:5) is a phrase from the Gospels that seems to jump out at you. To cooperate with divine grace means to be light to those who hurt and are in darkness—the darkness of depression or poverty, the darkness of sin or addiction. You are light.

You are part of the ever-singing song that is the Mass. You are in communion with all Catholics who were, who are, and who ever will be. This holy and sacred mystery cannot be understood with words but must be experienced in the heart. Come to Mass with the proper disposition, listen to your own voice, and cooperate with the divine grace offered to you.

Chapter 13
A Four-Week Psalter

The Form of Prayer in the Liturgy of the Hours

The Prayer of the Church

The Liturgy of the Hours is your prayer! It is the prayer the Church has given to all Christians. This is what the Church says to us about prayer:

> Jesus has commanded us to do as he did. On many occasions, he said: "pray" (Matthew 6:6), "ask" (Matthew 7:7), "in my name" (John 14:13).

We are the Body of Christ. We are his hands, his feet, and his voice. In the Liturgy of the Hours, we, as one member of the Body of Christ, join ourselves in spirit and voice to the entire Body of Christ throughout the world as we pray, ask, and seek with Jesus, our leader. Because it is the prayer of the Church, the Liturgy of the Hours is best prayed with others. We can also pray it alone, because it offers a good way to structure our daily prayer. We can join with friends to pray, when possible. Know, however, that when we pray alone, the saints and Christians throughout the world join us.

The Psalter provided here is an adaptation of this form of prayer, written especially for young people to use once a day. It is offered as an introduction to this form of prayer. The actual Liturgy of the Hours includes prayers for morning and evening, in a form that is similar to the one described here.

Structure of the Prayer

Call to Prayer

We make the sign of the cross and pray for God to be near us and help us as we continue our prayer.

God, come to my assistance.
Lord, make haste to help me.
Glory to the Father, and to the Son, and to the Holy Spirit:
as it was in the beginning, is now, and will be forever. Amen.

Antiphon

Notice a phrase that is said before the Psalm and then repeated after it. This phrase is called the antiphon (AN-ti-fohn). It is said and then repeated to show the character of the Psalm or to highlight an important line in it that otherwise might be overlooked. By saying the antiphon in the beginning, we can know what is important in the Psalm. By saying it at the end, it reminds us of what we just prayed.

Psalm

The Psalms are God's word. Humans wrote them under the inspiration of the Holy Spirit. They are a gift from God to us. As people who have received God's blessings, we feel the need to praise and seek God or to ask for God's forgiveness. The Psalms are God's gift to us to help us voice our feelings to God.

The Psalms were Jesus's prayer book. They have been the Christian prayer book for two thousand years, and they remain the prayer book of Christians today. Imagine, every time we pray one of the Psalms, someone is praying them with us. We are joining our voice with countless Christians in making a gift to God.

Scripture Reading and Response to the Reading

Liturgical prayer is a conversation or a dialogue between God and God's people. God speaks. We listen. We respond. God listens. God responds. This is the pattern of the Liturgy of the Hours. We speak our feelings to God in the Psalm, and then God responds by speaking to us in the Scripture reading. The Scriptures are God's response to us as individuals and as a Church.

After we have heard God's voice, we again voice our feelings to God in the response to the reading.

Gospel Canticle and Antiphon

Three great hymns of praise appear in Luke's Gospel: the Canticle of Zechariah (1:68–79), the Canticle of Mary (1:46–55), and the Canticle of Simeon (2:29–32). All the Scriptures are inspired by the Holy Spirit, but Catholics hold the Gospels to be particularly important because they are the stories of Jesus. Because these hymns of praise are from the Gospels, Catholics pray them daily—the Canticle of Zechariah in the morning and the Canticle of Mary in the evening.

Antiphon

I am always safe with you, my Lord; you are all I need in life.

Scripture Reading

Romans 11:25,30–36

So that you may not claim to be wiser than you are, brothers and sisters, I want you to understand this mystery: . . . Just as you were once disobedient to God but have now received mercy because of their disobedience, so they have now been disobedient in order that, by the mercy shown to you, they too may now receive mercy. For God has imprisoned all in disobedience so that he may be merciful to all.

O the depth of the riches and wisdom and knowledge of God! How unsearchable are his judgments and how inscrutable his ways!

"For who has known the mind of the Lord?
Or who has been his counselor?"
"Or who has given a gift to him,
to receive a gift in return?"
For from him and through him and to him are all things. To him be the glory forever. Amen.

Prayer Response to the Reading

- My heart is filled with joy as I contemplate your works, O Lord.
- I celebrate the wisdom that brought all things into being, as I contemplate your works, O Lord.
- Glory to the Father, and to the Son, and to the Holy Spirit.
- My heart is filled with joy as I contemplate your works, O Lord.

Gospel Canticle

Antiphon

It is the Lamb of God, who takes away the sins of the world.

Canticle

- If you are praying in the morning, pray the morning canticle found at the end of chapter 13.
- If you are praying in the evening, pray the evening canticle found at the end of chapter 13.

Glory to the Father, and to the Son, and to the Holy Spirit:
as it was in the beginning, is now, and will be forever. Amen.

Antiphon

It is the Lamb of God, who takes away the sins of the world.

Intercession

Petitions

Giving all glory and honor to the God who loves us, we ask for help as we pray: *Be with me, Lord.*

- God of mercy, shower the world with your love so that all may dwell in your peace, we pray. *Be with me, Lord.*
- God of compassion, look with kindness on those who are hurting, alone, and scared. Show them the compassion they need, we pray. *Be with me, Lord.*
- God of wisdom, guide the actions of those who lead us to words of peace and prosperity for all, we pray. *Be with me, Lord.*
- God of glory, reward with eternal life all those you have called to be with you, we pray. *Be with me, Lord.*
- God of strength, throughout the coming week, give us the strength to do what we know is right, we pray. *Be with me, Lord.*

- God of love, help us answer your call to us and serve you with all of our hearts, we pray. *Be with me, Lord.*

Please take time to add your own needs and concerns.

Lord's Prayer

Let us pray in the perfect words taught to us by Jesus:
Our Father . . .

Closing Prayer

Always-present God, your watch reaches to all the ends of the earth. Even the pull of sin cannot stop your loving plans. Help us receive your embrace and give us the strength to follow you and to reflect peace to those we meet. We ask this in the name of Jesus, the Lord, and with the power of the Holy Spirit. Amen.

Dismissal

May the Lord bless us and protect us from evil and bring us to the joy of heaven. Amen.

Monday, Week 1

Call to Prayer

God, come to my assistance.
Lord, make haste to help me.
Glory to the Father, and to the
    Son, and to the Holy Spirit:
as it was in the beginning, is
    now, and will be forever.
    Amen.

Psalm

Antiphon

Worship the Lord in all his
glory.

Psalm 29

Ascribe to the LORD, O heavenly
    beings,
ascribe to the LORD glory and
    strength.
Ascribe to the LORD the glory of
    his name;
worship the LORD in holy splen-
    dor.
The voice of the LORD is over
    the waters;
the God of glory thunders, the
    LORD, over mighty waters.

The voice of the LORD is power-
    ful;
the voice of the LORD is full of
    majesty.
The voice of the LORD breaks
    the cedars;
the LORD breaks the cedars of
    Lebanon.
He makes Lebanon skip like a
    calf,
and Sirion like a young wild ox.
The voice of the LORD flashes
    forth flames of fire.
The voice of the LORD shakes
    the wilderness;
the LORD shakes the wilderness
    of Kadesh.
The voice of the LORD causes the
    oaks to whirl,
and strips the forest bare; and in
    his temple all say, "Glory!"
The LORD sits enthroned over
    the flood;
the LORD sits enthroned as king
    forever.
May the LORD give strength to
    his people!
May the LORD bless his people
    with peace!

Glory to the Father, and to the
Son, and to the Holy Spirit:
as it was in the beginning, is
now, and will be forever.
Amen.

Psalm Prayer

Mighty God, your power is
greater than any known in the
world. Help us always to see
your strength at work in the
world, Lord, through others and
through ourselves.

Antiphon

Worship the Lord in all his
glory.

Scripture Reading

Colossians 1:9–13

For this reason, since the day we
heard it, we have not ceased praying for you and asking that you
may be filled with the knowledge
of God's will in all spiritual wisdom and understanding, so that
you may lead lives worthy of the
Lord, fully pleasing to him, as you
bear fruit in every good work and
as you grow in the knowledge of
God. May you be made strong
with all the strength that comes
from his glorious power, and may
you be prepared to endure everything with patience, while joyfully
giving thanks to the Father, who
has enabled you to share in the
inheritance of the saints in the
light. He has rescued us from
the power of darkness and trans-
ferred us into the kingdom of his
beloved Son.

Prayer Response to the Reading

- Only you can rescue me, Lord,
  because my sins have brought
  you sadness.
- Please have mercy on me in
  my weakness, because my sins
  have brought you sadness.
- Glory to the Father, and to
  the Son, and to the Holy
  Spirit.
- Only you can rescue me, Lord,
  because my sins have brought
  you sadness.

Gospel Canticle

Antiphon

Lord, if you will it, you can heal me. And Jesus said: "I do; you are healed."

Canticle

- If you are praying in the morning, pray the morning canticle found at the end of chapter 13.
- If you are praying in the evening, pray the evening canticle found at the end of chapter 13.

Glory to the Father, and to the Son, and to the Holy Spirit:
as it was in the beginning, is now, and will be forever. Amen.

Antiphon

Lord, if you will it, you can heal me. And Jesus said: "I do; you are healed."

Intercession

Petitions

God has made a covenant with us that will never end. In gratitude for all the gifts the Lord gives us, we pray: *Lord, bless your people.*

- Give our leaders the wisdom and courage to make decisions for the good of all people, we pray. *Lord, bless your people.*
- Give those who hunger, food; those who hurt, comfort; and those who suffer, relief, we pray. *Lord, bless your people.*
- Give those who have died a place with you in heaven, we pray. *Lord, bless your people.*
- Give us the courage to lead lives that are signs of you in this world, we pray. *Lord, bless your people.*
- Give us the patience to deal with the hassles that come our way, we pray. *Lord, bless your people.*
- Give our hearts the peace that only you can give us, we pray. *Lord, bless your people.*

Please take time to add your own needs and concerns.

Lord's Prayer

Let us pray in the perfect words
taught to us by Jesus:
Our Father . . .

Closing Prayer

Heavenly Father, may our desire
to serve you bring us closer to you.
Hear the prayer of those who work
so hard to follow your call in this
world. Open all eyes to see what is
possible through you. We ask this
in the name of Jesus, your Son and
our Lord, and with the power of
the Holy Spirit. Amen.

Dismissal

May the Lord bless us and protect
us from evil and bring us to the
joy of heaven. Amen.

Tuesday, Week 1

Call to Prayer

God, come to my assistance.
Lord, make haste to help me.
Glory to the Father, and to the
Son, and to the Holy Spirit:
as it was in the beginning, is
now, and will be forever.
Amen.

Psalm

Antiphon

The one who has a pure and
humble heart will climb God's
mountain.

Psalm 24

The earth is the LORD's and all
that is in it,
the world, and those who live
in it;
for he has founded it on the seas,
and established it on the rivers.

Who shall ascend the hill of the
LORD?
And who shall stand in his holy
place?

Those who have clean hands and
pure hearts,
who do not lift up their souls to
what is false,
and do not swear deceitfully.

They will receive blessing from
the LORD,
and vindication from the God of
their salvation.

Such is the company of those
who seek him,
who seek the face of the God of
Jacob.

Lift up your heads, O gates!
and be lifted up, O ancient
doors!
that the King of glory may come
in.

Who is the King of glory?
The LORD, strong and mighty,
the LORD, mighty in battle.

Lift up your heads, O gates!
and be lifted up, O ancient
doors!
that the King of glory may come
in.

Who is this King of glory?
The LORD of hosts,
he is the King of glory.

Glory to the Father, and to the
   Son, and to the Holy Spirit:
as it was in the beginning, is
   now, and will be forever.
   Amen.

Psalm Prayer

Make us ready to welcome you
when you come again in glory.
Free us from sin, protect us from
evil, and make us worthy to live
forever in your presence.

Antiphon

The one who has a pure and
humble heart will climb God's
mountain.

Scripture Reading

1 John 3:1–3

See what love the Father has
given us, that we should be
called children of God; and that
is what we are. The reason the
world does not know us is that it
did not know him. Beloved, we
are God's children now; what we
will be has not yet been revealed.
What we do know is this: when
he is revealed, we will be like
him, for we will see him as he is.
And all who have this hope in
him purify themselves, just as he
is pure.

Prayer Response to the Reading

- Your promise to us remains
  strong forever.
- The new covenant you made
  with us remains strong forever.
- Glory to the Father, and to
  the Son, and to the Holy
  Spirit.
- Your promise to us remains
  strong forever.

Gospel Canticle

Antiphon

To truly be a child of God, pray
for those who speak against you
and your family.

Canticle

- If you are praying in the morning, pray the morning canticle
  found at the end of chapter 13.
- If you are praying in the evening, pray the evening canticle
  found at the end of chapter 13.

Glory to the Father, and to the
   Son, and to the Holy Spirit:
as it was in the beginning, is
   now, and will be forever.
   Amen.

Antiphon

To truly be a child of God, pray for those who speak against you and your family.

Intercession

Petitions

Let us give praise to Christ, the Lord, who came to live among us and still does to this day as we pray: *Lord, hear our prayer.*

- Ruler of glory, show the rulers of our world how to rule with hearts of service, we pray. *Lord, hear our prayer.*
- Let daughters and sons learn from the example of your love and respect for your parents, we pray. *Lord, hear our prayer.*
- Free those trapped by oppression and hatred and guide them to the safety only you can bring, we pray. *Lord, hear our prayer.*
- Accept all who have left this world in your friendship and give them peace, we pray. *Lord, hear our prayer.*

- Make our hearts compassionate, as we struggle to be kind to those who hurt us, we pray. *Lord, hear our prayer.*
- Help us know you and love you in all we do and say, we pray. *Lord, hear our prayer.*

Please take time to add your own needs and concerns.

Lord's Prayer

Let us pray in the perfect words taught to us by Jesus:
Our Father . . .

Closing Prayer

Loving Father, thank you for the gift of being one of your children. May our prayers to you and our work in your name bring you joy and bring more people into your family of love. We ask this through our Lord, Jesus Christ, your Son, who lives and reigns with you in the unity of the Holy Spirit, one God, forever and ever. Amen.

Dismissal

May the Lord bless us and protect us from evil and bring us to the joy of heaven. Amen.

Wednesday, Week 1

Call to Prayer

God, come to my assistance.
Lord, make haste to help me.
Glory to the Father, and to the
    Son, and to the Holy Spirit:
as it was in the beginning, is
    now, and will be forever.
    Amen.

Psalm

Antiphon

God is here, sing out in praise.

Psalm 47

Clap your hands, all you peoples;
shout to God with loud songs
    of joy.
For the LORD, the Most High, is
    awesome,
a great king over all the earth.

He subdued peoples under us,
and nations under our feet.
He chose our heritage for us,
the pride of Jacob whom he
    loves.

God has gone up with a shout,
the LORD with the sound of a
    trumpet.
Sing praises to God, sing praises;
sing praises to our King, sing
    praises.

For God is the king of all the
    earth;
sing praises with a psalm.
God is king over the nations;
God sits on his holy throne.

The princes of the peoples gather
as the people of the God of
    Abraham.
For the shields of the earth
    belong to God;
he is highly exalted.

Glory to the Father, and to the
    Son, and to the Holy Spirit:
as it was in the beginning, is
    now, and will be forever.
    Amen.

Psalm Prayer

We celebrate your name as we
sing with all of our hearts. May
our voices always remember how
you brought us to a new life in
you.

Antiphon

God is here, sing out in praise.

Scripture Reading

Tobit 4:15,16,18–19

And what you hate, do not do to anyone. . . . Give some of your food to the hungry, and some of your clothing to the naked. . . . Seek advice from every wise person and do not despise any useful counsel. At all times bless the Lord God, and ask him that your ways may be made straight and that all your paths and plans may prosper.

Prayer Response to the Reading

- Lead my heart closer to your will, my God.
- Guide my steps along the path, closer to your will, my God.
- Glory to the Father, and to the Son, and to the Holy Spirit.
- Lead my heart closer to your will, my God.

Gospel Canticle

Antiphon

Seek the kingdom of God first of all, and everything else will be given to you.

Canticle

- If you are praying in the morning, pray the morning canticle found at the end of chapter 13.
- If you are praying in the evening, pray the evening canticle found at the end of chapter 13.

Glory to the Father, and to the Son, and to the Holy Spirit:
as it was in the beginning, is now, and will be forever. Amen.

Antiphon

Seek the kingdom of God first of all, and everything else will be given to you.

Intercession

Petitions

In everything we do and say, God should be praised, because we are surrounded by his love. As chosen people, we pray: *Show us your love.*

- Remember your Church, the Church that wants nothing more than to see your face, we pray. *Show us your love.*
- Let all the countries come to see you as the one true path to happiness, we pray. *Show us your love.*
- Give our brothers and sisters all they truly need, we pray. *Show us your love.*
- Open the doors of heaven to those who have passed on, and show them mercy, we pray. *Show us your love.*
- Keep us in the right path, and may our actions always be focused on you, we pray. *Show us your love.*
- Take away any anger and jealousy that leads us to hurt those around us, we pray. *Show us your love.*

Please take time to add your own needs and concerns.

Lord's Prayer

Let us pray in the perfect words taught to us by Jesus:
Our Father . . .

Closing Prayer

God, our provider, always watch over us. In the middle of all that burdens us in this life, give us the strength and love to continue using your name. We ask this in the name of Jesus, the Lord, and with the power of the Holy Spirit. Amen.

Dismissal

May the Lord bless us and protect us from evil and bring us to the joy of heaven. Amen.

Thursday, Week 1

Call to Prayer

God, come to my assistance.
Lord, make haste to help me.
Glory to the Father, and to the
    Son, and to the Holy Spirit:
as it was in the beginning, is
    now, and will be forever.
    Amen.

Psalm

Antiphon

Sing out to our glorious God in
heaven.

Psalm 57

Be merciful to me, O God, be
    merciful to me,
for in you my soul takes refuge;
in the shadow of your wings I
    will take refuge,
until the destroying storms pass
    by.

I cry to God Most High, to God
    who fulfills his purpose for
    me.
He will send from heaven and
    save me,

he will put to shame those who
    trample on me.
God will send forth his steadfast
    love and his faithfulness.

I lie down among lions
that greedily devour human prey;
their teeth are spears and arrows,
their tongues sharp swords.

Be exalted, O God, above the
    heavens.
Let your glory be over all the
    earth.

They set a net for my steps;
my soul was bowed down.
They dug a pit in my path,
but they have fallen into it
    themselves.

My heart is steadfast, O God,
my heart is steadfast.
I will sing and make melody.

Awake, my soul! Awake, O harp
    and lyre!
I will awake the dawn.
I will give thanks to you, O
    Lord, among the peoples;
I will sing praises to you among
    the nations.

For your steadfast love is as high
    as the heavens;

your faithfulness extends to the clouds.
Be exalted, O God, above the heavens.
Let your glory be over all the earth.

Glory to the Father, and to the Son, and to the Holy Spirit:
as it was in the beginning, is now, and will be forever. Amen.

Psalm Prayer

Rescue us from the grasping hands of evil by showing to all people your mercy and truth. We can then spread your name to all peoples as companions on the journey.

Antiphon

Sing out to our glorious God in heaven.

Scripture Reading

1 Peter 1:6–9

In this you rejoice, even if now for a little while you have had to suffer various trials, so that the genuineness of your faith—being more precious than gold that, though perishable, is tested by fire—may be found to result in praise and glory and honor when Jesus Christ is revealed. Although you have not seen him, you love him; and even though you do not see him now, you believe in him and rejoice with an indescribable and glorious joy, for you are receiving the outcome of your faith, the salvation of your souls.

Prayer Response to the Reading

- My heart cries out to you; hear my plea, O Lord.
- I will do what you ask of me, hear my plea, O Lord.
- Glory to the Father, and to the Son, and to the Holy Spirit.
- My heart cries out to you; hear my plea, O Lord.

Gospel Canticle

Antiphon

Whoever does the will of God is a true member of my family.

Canticle

- If you are praying in the morning, pray the morning canticle found at the end of chapter 13.

- If you are praying in the evening, pray the evening canticle found at the end of chapter 13.

Glory to the Father, and to the Son, and to the Holy Spirit:
as it was in the beginning, is now, and will be forever. Amen.

Antiphon

Whoever does the will of God is a true member of my family.

Intercession

Petitions

All our hope is in our God, who gives us help. With this hope and faith, we pray: *Bless your children, O source of life.*

- Keep us always aware of the love you have for us and the works you do for us, we pray. *Bless your children, O source of life.*
- Let those who lead your Church bring us together and be your tools for good work, we pray. *Bless your children, O source of life.*
- As your children, give us patience with those who test our faith, we pray. *Bless your children, O source of life.*
- Take care of your children you have already brought into your loving presence, we pray. *Bless your children, O source of life.*
- Help us keep a childlike heart and not let evil bring us down, we pray. Bless your children, *O source of life.*
- Give us the faith to serve you in the way you are calling us to serve, we pray. *Bless your children, O source of life.*

Please take time to add your own needs and concerns.

Lord's Prayer

Let us pray in the perfect words taught to us by Jesus:
Our Father . . .

Closing Prayer

Ancient of Days, we, your adopted sons and daughters, pray to you. Keep us safe in the darkness as we look for the light of truth, your Son, Jesus Christ, who lives and reigns with you and the Holy Spirit, one God, forever and ever. Amen.

Dismissal

May the Lord bless us and protect us from evil and bring us to the joy of heaven. Amen.

Friday, Week 1

Call to Prayer

God, come to my assistance.
Lord, make haste to help me.
Glory to the Father, and to the
Son, and to the Holy Spirit:
as it was in the beginning, is
now, and will be forever. Amen.

Psalm

Antiphon

Go before our Lord and God
singing with happy hearts.

Psalm 51

Have mercy on me, O God,
    according to your steadfast
    love;
according to your abundant
    mercy blot out my transgres-
    sions.
Wash me thoroughly from my
    iniquity,
and cleanse me from my sin.

For I know my transgressions,
and my sin is ever before me.

Against you, you alone, have I
    sinned,
and done what is evil in your
    sight,
so that you are justified in your
    sentence
and blameless when you pass
    judgment.
Indeed, I was born guilty,
a sinner when my mother
    conceived me.

You desire truth in the inward
    being;
therefore teach me wisdom in
    my secret heart.
Purge me with hyssop, and I
    shall be clean;
wash me, and I shall be whiter
    than snow.

Let me hear joy and gladness;
let the bones that you have
    crushed rejoice.
Hide your face from my sins,
and blot out all my iniquities.
Create in me a clean heart, O
    God,
and put a new and right spirit
    within me.
Do not cast me away from your
    presence,
and do not take your holy spirit
    from me.

Restore to me the joy of your
  salvation,
and sustain in me a willing
  spirit.
Then I will teach transgressors
  your ways,
and sinners will return to you.

Deliver me from bloodshed, O
  God, O God of my salvation,
and my tongue will sing aloud of
  your deliverance.
O Lord, open my lips,
and my mouth will declare your
  praise.

For you have no delight in
  sacrifice;
if I were to give a burnt offering,
  you would not be pleased.
The sacrifice acceptable to God
  is a broken spirit;
a broken and contrite heart, O
  God, you will not despise.

Do good to Zion in your good
  pleasure;
rebuild the walls of Jerusalem,
then you will delight in right
  sacrifices,
in burnt offerings and whole
  burnt offerings;
then bulls will be offered on
  your altar.

Glory to the Father, and to the
  Son, and to the Holy Spirit:
as it was in the beginning, is
  now, and will be forever.
  Amen.

Psalm Prayer

With all of our hearts, we call
to you and ask you to open our
hearts to announce your good
news.

Antiphon

Go before our Lord and God,
singing with happy hearts.

Scripture Reading

Ephesians 4:29–32

Let no evil talk come out of your
mouths, but only what is useful
for building up, as there is need,
so that your words may give
grace to those who hear. And
do not grieve the Holy Spirit
of God, with which you were
marked with a seal for the day
of redemption. Put away from
you all bitterness and wrath and
anger and wrangling and slander,
together with all malice, and
be kind to one another, tender-
hearted, forgiving one another,
as God in Christ has forgiven
you.

Prayer Response to the Reading

- Christ forgives us and cleanses us of our sins with his blood.
- A nation of people to lead and serve, with his blood.
- Glory to the Father, and to the Son, and to the Holy Spirit.
- Christ forgives us and cleanses us of our sins with his blood.

Gospel Canticle

Antiphon

Whatever it is you do, do it in the name of Jesus Christ.

Canticle

- If you are praying in the morning, pray the morning canticle found at the end of chapter 13.
- If you are praying in the evening, pray the evening canticle found at the end of chapter 13.

Glory to the Father, and to the Son, and to the Holy Spirit:
as it was in the beginning, is now, and will be forever. Amen.

Antiphon

Whatever it is you do, do it in the name of Jesus Christ.

Intercession

Petitions

Through the cross, Jesus brought salvation to the people. In amazement at this selfless act, we pray: *Be with me, Lamb of God.*

- Upon the cross, Jesus offered the perfect sacrifice, so for all those who suffer without God's love, we pray. *Be with me, Lamb of God.*
- Set free those unjustly imprisoned. Bring to good health those who are sick and injured, we pray. *Be with me, Lamb of God.*
- Cover us, your people, in the armor of salvation that protects us from the deceptions of sin, we pray. *Be with me, Lamb of God.*
- Lead the departed into the light of your dwelling place to look upon you forever, we pray. *Be with me, Lamb of God.*
- Help us see that the Lord is at our side in the struggles and problems of our daily life, we pray. *Be with me, Lamb of God.*

- May our words build up our friends and family and not drag them down, we pray. *Be with me, Lamb of God.*

Please take time to add your own needs and concerns.

Lord's Prayer

Let us pray in the perfect words taught to us by Jesus:
Our Father . . .

Closing Prayer

God, our source of life, help us follow the example of Jesus, sharing the burden he carries for us, bearing all wrongs patiently. Through these acts, may we come to share in his glory in the kingdom where he lives with you and the Holy Spirit, one God, forever and ever. Amen.

Dismissal

May the Lord bless us and protect us from evil and bring us to the joy of heaven. Amen.

Saturday, Week 1

Call to Prayer

God, come to my assistance.
Lord, make haste to help me.
Glory to the Father, and to the
    Son, and to the Holy Spirit:
as it was in the beginning, is
    now, and will be forever.
    Amen.

Psalm 113

Antiphon

Blessed are you, Mary ever virgin, for you carried the Creator of the world in your womb.

Psalm 113

Praise the LORD! Praise, O servants of the LORD;
praise the name of the LORD.
Blessed be the name of the LORD
from this time on and forevermore.

From the rising of the sun to its setting
the name of the LORD is to be praised.

The LORD is high above all
    nations,
and his glory above the heavens.

Who is like the LORD our God,
who is seated on high,
who looks far down
on the heavens and the earth?

He raises the poor from the dust,
and lifts the needy from the ash
    heap,
to make them sit with princes,
with the princes of his people.

He gives the barren woman a
    home,
making her the joyous mother of
    children.
Praise the LORD!

Glory to the Father, and to the
    Son, and to the Holy Spirit:
as it was in the beginning, is
    now, and will be forever.
    Amen.

Psalm Prayer

The Mighty One was blessed
by Mary's act of trust and love.
We pray that our actions in our
lives can also praise the Lord our
God.

Antiphon

Blessed are you, Mary ever virgin, for you carried the Creator of the world in your womb.

Scripture Reading

Isaiah 61:10

I will greatly rejoice in the LORD,
   my whole being shall exult in
   my God;
for he has clothed me with the
      garments of salvation,
   he has covered me with the
   robe of righteousness,
as a bridegroom decks himself
   with a garland,
      and as a bride adorns herself
      with her jewels.

Prayer Response to the Reading

- Hail Mary, full of grace, the Lord is with you.
- Blessed are you among women, and blessed is the fruit of your womb. The Lord is with you.
- Glory to the Father, and to the Son, and to the Holy Spirit.
- Hail Mary, full of grace, the Lord is with you.

Gospel Canticle

Antiphon

You are the glory of Jerusalem, the joy of Israel, the most honored of your people.

Canticle

- If you are praying in the morning, pray the morning canticle found at the end of chapter 13.
- If you are praying in the evening, pray the evening canticle found at the end of chapter 13.

Glory to the Father, and to the Son, and to the Holy Spirit:
as it was in the beginning, is now, and will be forever. Amen.

Antiphon

You are the glory of Jerusalem, the joy of Israel, the most honored of your people.

Intercession

Petitions

Let us give thanks to Jesus, our Savior, who chose the Virgin Mary for his mother. With courage, we pray: *May your mother intercede for us, Jesus, our Savior.*

- By your redeeming power, you preserved your mother from all stain of sin. Keep watch over your people and lead us from sin, we pray. *May your mother intercede for us, Jesus, our Savior.*
- Mary was pure and immaculate as the sanctuary of the Holy Spirit. Help make us worthy of your gifts, we pray. *May your mother intercede for us, Jesus, our Savior.*
- You taught Mary to choose your will. Give us the wisdom to imitate her perfect example, we pray. *May your mother intercede for us, Jesus, our Savior.*
- You crowned Mary as Queen of Heaven and set her next to you. Grant us a share in this glory, we pray. *May your mother intercede for us, Jesus, our Savior.*
- Mary did not let her world influence her decision to be your mother. Give us the courage not to let our world influence us in serving you, we pray. *May your mother intercede for us, Jesus, our Savior.*
- Though very young, Mary responded when you called. Help us respond to you and not let our age or other concerns worry us, we pray. *May*

your mother intercede for us, Jesus, our Savior.

Please take time to add your own needs and concerns.

Lord's Prayer

Let us pray in the perfect words taught to us by Jesus:
Our Father . . .

Closing Prayer

God of mercy, give us strength. May we who honor the memory of the Mother of God rise above the sins and failings of the past with the help of her prayers and example. Grant this through our Lord, Jesus Christ, your Son, who lives and reigns with you and the Holy Spirit, one God, forever and ever. Amen.

Dismissal

May the Lord bless us and protect us from evil and bring us to the joy of heaven. Amen.

Sunday, Week 2

Call to Prayer

God, come to my assistance.
Lord, make haste to help me.
Glory to the Father, and to the
    Son, and to the Holy Spirit:
as it was in the beginning, is
    now, and will be forever.
    Amen.

Psalm

Antiphon

Praise the Lord's never-ending
greatness in song.

Psalm 150

Praise the LORD! Praise God in
    his sanctuary;
praise him in his mighty
    firmament!
Praise him for his mighty deeds;
praise him according to his
    surprising greatness!

Praise him with trumpet sound;
praise him with lute and harp!
Praise him with tambourine and
    dance;
praise him with strings and pipe!
Praise him with clanging cym-
    bals;
praise him with loud clashing
    cymbals!
Let everything that breathes
    praise the LORD!
Praise the LORD!

Glory to the Father, and to the
    Son, and to the Holy Spirit:
as it was in the beginning, is
    now, and will be forever.
    Amen.

Psalm Prayer

God of triumph, everything you
do is worthy of our thanks and
praise. May all our songs be sung
from our hearts and be just the
beginning of endless gratitude
for your love.

Antiphon

Praise the Lord's never-ending
greatness in song.

Scripture Reading

Ezekiel 36:25–28

I will sprinkle clean water upon you, and you shall be clean from all your uncleannesses, and from all your idols I will cleanse you. A new heart I will give you, and a new spirit I will put within you; and I will remove from your body the heart of stone and give you a heart of flesh. And I will put my spirit within you, and make you follow in my statutes and be careful to observe my ordinances. Then you shall live in the land that I gave to your ancestors; and you shall be my people, and I will be your God.

Prayer Response to the Reading

- Give me a heart pure and clean, my God.
- In place of a heart hardened by hate and sin pure and clean, my God.
- Glory to the Father, and to the Son, and to the Holy Spirit.
- Give me a heart pure and clean, my God.

Gospel Canticle

Antiphon

Where you keep your treasures, you also keep your heart.

Canticle

- If you are praying in the morning, pray the morning canticle found at the end of chapter 13.
- If you are praying in the evening, pray the evening canticle found at the end of chapter 13.

Glory to the Father, and to the Son, and to the Holy Spirit:
as it was in the beginning, is now, and will be forever. Amen.

Antiphon

Where you keep your treasures, you also keep your heart.

Intercession

Petitions

Let us praise and honor Jesus, our Savior, who died and rose again in glory. Praising him, let us pray: *Raise us up, victorious Savior.*

- Give guidance to those who lead your Church in word and action and lift them up as an example for all, we pray. *Raise us up, victorious Savior.*
- Give peace to those who are sick and suffering and help them rise above their weaknesses, we pray. *Raise us up, victorious Savior.*
- Give faith to those who do not believe in your boundless love and bring them up from the fear and confusion that keeps them down, we pray. *Raise us up, victorious Savior.*
- Give patience to us this week as we try to live as you called us and lift us above all that may get in our way, we pray. *Raise us up, victorious Savior.*
- Give healing to those we may have hurt with our own words and actions and pull us up from our sinful ways, we pray. *Raise us up, victorious Savior.*
- Give mercy to those who have died and raise them up on the last day, we pray. *Raise us up, victorious Savior.*

Please take time to add your own needs and concerns.

Lord's Prayer

Let us pray in the perfect words taught to us by Jesus:
Our Father . . .

Closing Prayer

Almighty Father, your love is more than we can ever imagine. Fill our hearts with your love, our thoughts with your wisdom, and our mouths with your words, so that our entire lives may be a part of your plan. We ask this in the name of Jesus, the Lord, and with the power of the Holy Spirit. Amen.

Dismissal

May the Lord bless us and protect us from evil and bring us to the joy of heaven. Amen.

Monday, Week 2

Call to Prayer

God, come to my assistance.
Lord, make haste to help me.
Glory to the Father, and to the
Son, and to the Holy Spirit:
as it was in the beginning, is
now, and will be forever.
Amen.

Psalm

Antiphon

All of heaven echoes with your
praises, O Lord.

Psalm 19:1–6

The heavens are telling the glory
of God;
and the firmament proclaims his
handiwork.
Day to day pours forth speech,
and night to night declares
knowledge.

There is no speech, nor are there
words; their voice is not heard;
yet their voice goes out through
all the earth,
and their words to the end of the
world.

In the heavens he has set a tent
for the sun,
which comes out like a
bridegroom from his
wedding canopy,
and like a strong man runs its
course with joy.

Its rising is from the end of the
heavens,
and its circuit to the end of
them;
and nothing is hid from its heat.

Glory to the Father, and to the
Son, and to the Holy Spirit:
as it was in the beginning, is
now, and will be forever.
Amen.

Psalm Prayer

Glorious God, all you have done
for your people is amazing and
beyond approach. May we always
honor your love for us with
praise of your name.

Antiphon

All of heaven echoes with your
praises, O Lord.

Scripture Reading

1 Thessalonians 2:11–13

As you know, we dealt with each one of you like a father with his children, urging and encouraging you and pleading that you lead a life worthy of God, who calls you into his own kingdom and glory.

We also constantly give thanks to God for this, that when you received the word of God that you heard from us, you accepted it not as a human word but as what it really is, God's word, which is also at work in you believers.

Prayer Response to the Reading

- Lord, hear my prayer that rises up to you.
- Like incense burning before you, that rises up to you.
- Glory to the Father, and to the Son, and to the Holy Spirit.
- Lord, hear my prayer that rises up to you.

Gospel Canticle

Antiphon

A great prophet has come to us, and God is in our midst.

Canticle

- If you are praying in the morning, pray the morning canticle found at the end of chapter 13.
- If you are praying in the evening, pray the evening canticle found at the end of chapter 13.

Glory to the Father, and to the
    Son, and to the Holy Spirit:
as it was in the beginning, is
    now, and will be forever.
    Amen.

Antiphon

A great prophet has come to us, and God is in our midst.

Intercession

Petitions

Our savior has made us holy, a people set apart to do his will. With that in mind, we call out in prayer: *Hear your people, O Holy One.*

- Remember your Church throughout the world and continue to bless it and keep it safe, we pray. *Hear your people, O Holy One.*
- Take care of the poor, the suffering, and those who are forced to go without basic needs, we pray. *Hear your people, O Holy One.*
- Move the hearts of those who refuse to know your love and compassion, we pray. *Hear your people, O Holy One.*
- Enable us to see you in others, even when they are least like you, we pray. *Hear your people, O Holy One.*
- Take our daily efforts to serve you as our prayer of thanks, we pray. *Hear your people, O Holy One.*
- Lead all souls to your heavenly kingdom, especially those most in need of your care, we pray. *Hear your people, O Holy One.*

Please take time to add your own needs and concerns.

Lord's Prayer

Let us pray in the perfect words taught to us by Jesus:
Our Father . . .

Closing Prayer

Father, you have blessed us with the opportunity to do your work. Give us what we need, keep us safe, and see what we do as honoring you for all you have done for us. We ask this through our Lord, Jesus Christ, your Son, who lives and reigns with you, in the unity of the Holy Spirit, one God, forever and ever. Amen.

Dismissal

May the Lord bless us and protect us from evil and bring us to the joy of heaven. Amen.

Tuesday, Week 2

Call to Prayer

God, come to my assistance.
Lord, make haste to help me.
Glory to the Father, and to the
    Son, and to the Holy Spirit:
as it was in the beginning, is
    now, and will be forever.
    Amen.

Psalm

Antiphon

You have come to the earth and
showered it with your rain to
bring forth its bounty.

Psalm 65

Praise is due to you,
O God, in Zion;
and to you shall vows be per-
    formed,
O you who answer prayer!

To you all flesh shall come.
When deeds of iniquity over-
    whelm us,
you forgive our transgressions.

Happy are those whom you
    choose
and bring near to live in your
    courts.
We shall be satisfied with the
    goodness of your house,
your holy temple.

By awesome deeds you answer us
    with deliverance,
O God of our salvation;
you are the hope of all the ends
    of the earth
and of the farthest seas.

By your strength you established
    the mountains;
you are girded with might.
You silence the roaring of the
    seas, the roaring of their
    waves,
the tumult of the peoples.

Those who live at earth's farthest
    bounds
are awed by your signs;
you make the gateways of the
    morning
and the evening shout for joy.

You visit the earth and water it,
you greatly enrich it;
the river of God is full of water;

you provide the people with
grain,
for so you have prepared it.

You water its furrows abundantly,
settling its ridges,
softening it with showers,
and blessing its growth.

You crown the year with your
bounty;
your wagon tracks overflow with
richness.

The pastures of the wilderness
overflow,
the hills gird themselves with
joy,
the meadows clothe themselves
with flocks,
the valleys deck themselves with
grain,
they shout and sing together for
joy.

Glory to the Father, and to the
Son, and to the Holy Spirit:
as it was in the beginning, is
now, and will be forever.
Amen.

Psalm Prayer

Like rain, pour your spirit out
upon us, Lord, and bless the
fruit of our work. Hear our
prayer and our praise of your
name.

Antiphon

You have come to the earth and
showered it with your rain to
bring forth its bounty.

Scripture Reading

1 Thessalonians 5:2–6

For you yourselves know very
well that the day of the Lord
will come like a thief in the
night. When they say, "There
is peace and security," then
sudden destruction will come
upon them, as labor pains come
upon a pregnant woman, and
there will be no escape! But you,
beloved, are not in darkness, for
that day to surprise you like a
thief; for you are all children of
light and children of the day;
we are not of the night or of
darkness. So then let us not fall
asleep as others do, but let us
keep awake and be sober.

Prayer Response
to the Reading

• I will know what true happiness is when I see you face to
face, my Lord.

- Contentment and never-ending peace with you, when I see you face to face, my Lord.
- Glory to the Father, and to the Son, and to the Holy Spirit.
- I will know what true happiness is when I see you face to face, my Lord.

Gospel Canticle

Antiphon

When the Son of Man comes among us, will he find faith in our hearts?

Canticle

- If you are praying in the morning, pray the morning canticle found at the end of chapter 13.
- If you are praying in the evening, pray the evening canticle found at the end of chapter 13.

Glory to the Father, and to the Son, and to the Holy Spirit:
as it was in the beginning, is now, and will be forever. Amen.

Antiphon

When the Son of Man comes among us, will he find faith in our hearts?

Intercession

Petitions

The Lord, our God, is the hope of the earth, hearing our prayers and praises. It is with this hope that we pray: *Lord, hear our prayer.*

- Guide the minds of world leaders to actions that will benefit all peoples, we pray. *Lord, hear our prayer.*
- Guide the hands of your sons and daughters to work for your glory and praise, we pray. *Lord, hear our prayer.*
- Guide the mouths of those who hate to speak words of kindness and forgiveness, we pray. *Lord, hear our prayer.*
- Guide our ears to hear you calling to us in the everyday events of our lives, we pray. *Lord, hear our prayer.*
- Guide the eyes of all to see you in all your glory, we pray. *Lord, hear our prayer.*
- Guide those who have left this world in your friendship into the true happiness of your presence, we pray. *Lord, hear our prayer.*

Please take time to add your own needs and concerns.

Lord's Prayer

Let us pray in the perfect words
taught to us by Jesus:
Our Father . . .

Closing Prayer

Almighty God, we await your
return by continuing to do your
will. Help us always to praise
you and bless you in all we do
and say. Remember our successes
and forgive our failures. We ask
this in the name of Jesus, the
Lord, and in the power of the
Holy Spirit. Amen.

Dismissal

May the Lord bless us and protect us from evil and bring us to
the joy of heaven. Amen.

Wednesday, Week 2

Call to Prayer

God, come to my assistance.
Lord, make haste to help me.
Glory to the Father, and to the
    Son, and to the Holy Spirit:
as it was in the beginning, is
    now, and will be forever.
    Amen.

Psalm

Antiphon

The Lord rules all the earth, let
all people be glad.

Psalm 97

The LORD is king! Let the earth
    rejoice;
let the many coastlands be glad!
Clouds and thick darkness are all
    around him;
righteousness and justice are the
    foundation of his throne.
Fire goes before him,
and consumes his adversaries on
    every side.
His lightnings light up the
    world;
the earth sees and trembles.

The mountains melt like wax
    before the LORD,
before the Lord of all the earth.
The heavens proclaim his
    righteousness;
and all the peoples behold his
    glory.
All worshipers of images are put
    to shame,
those who make their boast in
    worthless idols;
all gods bow down before him.

Zion hears and is glad, and the
    towns of Judah rejoice,
because of your judgments, O
    God.
For you, O LORD, are most high
    over all the earth;
you are exalted far above all
    gods.
The LORD loves those who hate
    evil;
he guards the lives of his faithful;
he rescues them from the hand
    of the wicked.
Light dawns for the righteous,
and joy for the upright in heart.

Rejoice in the LORD, O you
righteous,
and give thanks to his holy
name!

Glory to the Father, and to the
Son, and to the Holy Spirit:
as it was in the beginning, is
now, and will be forever.
Amen.

Psalm Prayer

Father, we see your incredible
power in the world you created
and your incredible love in the
way you treat your sons and
daughters. Do not forget your
love for us and continue to give
us everything we need today,
tomorrow, and forever.

Antiphon

The Lord rules all the earth, let
all people be glad.

Scripture Reading

Romans 8:35–39

Who will separate us from the
love of Christ? Will hardship,
or distress, or persecution, or
famine, or nakedness, or peril, or
sword? As it is written,

"For your sake we are being
killed all day long;
we are accounted as sheep
to be slaughtered."
No, in all these things we are
more than conquerors through
him who loved us. For I am
convinced that neither death,
nor life, nor angels, nor rulers,
nor things present, nor things to
come, nor powers, nor height,
nor depth, nor anything else in
all creation, will be able to separate us from the love of God in
Christ Jesus our Lord.

Prayer Response to the Reading

- I will praise the name of the
  Lord all the days of my life.
- From my mouth a song of
  praise, all the days of my life.
- Glory to the Father, and to
  the Son, and to the Holy
  Spirit.
- I will praise the name of the
  Lord all the days of my life.

Gospel Canticle

Antiphon

Your strong arm scatters the
prideful, and lifts up the humble.

Canticle

- If you are praying in the morning, pray the morning canticle found at the end of chapter 13.
- If you are praying in the evening, pray the evening canticle found at the end of chapter 13.

Glory to the Father, and to the
  Son, and to the Holy Spirit:
as it was in the beginning, is
  now, and will be forever.
  Amen.

Antiphon

Your strong arm scatters the prideful, and lifts up the humble.

Intercession

Petitions

Let us rejoice in God, for his pleasure comes from using his power to benefit his people. With this on our hearts, we pray: *Strengthen your people, God, our Savior.*

- Build up the faith of your people on earth, giving them hearts of service and minds always focused on you, we pray. *Strengthen your people, God, our Savior.*
- Give grace to the weak in mind, body, and spirit to overcome things that cause pain, we pray. *Strengthen your people, God, our Savior.*
- Protect all nature and all your creation from those who would harm it, we pray. *Strengthen your people, God, our Savior.*
- Grant us the ability to stand up for what we know is right and help us to live uprightly in what we say and do, we pray. *Strengthen your people, God, our Savior.*
- Use our daily actions as examples for others so they may see your goodness, we pray. *Strengthen your people, God, our Savior.*
- Give those who have gone before us a place with you in heaven, we pray. *Strengthen your people, God, our Savior.*

Please take time to add your own needs and concerns.

Lord's Prayer

Let us pray in the perfect words taught to us by Jesus:
Our Father . . .

Closing Prayer

Heavenly Father, you want nothing else but for us to be happy, and that happiness can be found only with you. Recognize our efforts this day to come closer to you and do not hold our setbacks against us. We ask this through our Lord, Jesus Christ, your Son, who lives and reigns with you, in the unity of the Holy Spirit, one God, forever and ever. Amen.

Dismissal

May the Lord bless us and protect us from evil and bring us to the joy of heaven. Amen.

Thursday, Week 2

Call to Prayer

God, come to my assistance.
Lord, make haste to help me.
Glory to the Father, and to the
    Son, and to the Holy Spirit:
as it was in the beginning, is
    now, and will be forever.
    Amen.

Psalm

Antiphon

Sing out in joy to God who is
the strength of his people.

Psalm 81

Sing aloud to God our strength;
shout for joy to the God of
Jacob.

Raise a song, sound the
    tambourine,
the sweet lyre with the harp.
Blow the trumpet at the new
    moon,
at the full moon, on our festal
    day.

For it is a statute for Israel,
an ordinance of the God of
    Jacob.

He made it a decree in Joseph,
when he went out over the land
    of Egypt.

I hear a voice I had not known:
"I relieved your shoulder of the
    burden;
your hands were freed from the
    basket.
In distress you called, and I
    rescued you;

I answered you in the secret
    place of thunder;
I tested you at the waters of
    Meribah.
Hear, O my people, while I
    admonish you;
O Israel, if you would but listen
    to me!

There shall be no strange god
    among you;
you shall not bow down to a
    foreign god.
I am the LORD your God,
who brought you up out of the
    land of Egypt.

Open your mouth wide and I
    will fill it.

"But my people did not listen to
    my voice;
Israel would not submit to me.
So I gave them over to their
    stubborn hearts,
to follow their own counsels.

O that my people would listen
    to me,
that Israel would walk in my ways!
Then I would quickly subdue
    their enemies,
and turn my hand against their
    foes.

Those who hate the LORD would
    cringe before him,
and their doom would last for-
    ever.
I would feed you with the finest
    of the wheat,
and with honey from the rock I
    would satisfy you."

Glory to the Father, and to the
    Son, and to the Holy Spirit:
as it was in the beginning, is
    now, and will be forever.
    Amen.

Psalm Prayer

Open our hearts, Lord, so that
we can give you praise. Help
us leave the temptation of sin
behind and fill our lives with
your love.

Antiphon

Sing out in joy to God who is
the strength of his people.

Scripture Reading

Romans 14:12–13,17–19

So then, each of us will be
accountable to God.

Let us therefore no longer pass
judgment on one another, but
resolve instead never to put a
stumbling block or hindrance in
the way of another. . . . For
the kingdom of God is not food
and drink but righteousness
and peace and joy in the Holy
Spirit. The one who thus serves
Christ is acceptable to God and
has human approval. Let us then
pursue what makes for peace and
for mutual upbuilding.

Prayer Response to the Reading

- Go out and tell all the world
  how wonderful God has been.
- Make known the blessings to
  all people how wonderful God
  has been.
- Glory to the Father, and to
  the Son, and to the Holy
  Spirit.

- Go out and tell all the world how wonderful God has been.

Gospel Canticle

Antiphon

If you want holiness, God can give you what you need, and more.

Canticle

- If you are praying in the morning, pray the morning canticle found at the end of chapter 13.
- If you are praying in the evening, pray the evening canticle found at the end of chapter 13.

Glory to the Father, and to the Son, and to the Holy Spirit:
as it was in the beginning, is now, and will be forever. Amen.

Antiphon

If you want holiness, God can give you what you need, and more.

Intercession

Petitions

Lift up your hearts to the Lord and give thanks for his many mercies and blessings. In this spirit of affection, we pray: *Have mercy and hear us.*

- Strengthen the Pope and bishops, who lead your people, and keep them safe from any harm, we pray. *Have mercy and hear us.*
- Protect our brothers and sisters who have no one to care for them and are in troubled situations, we pray. *Have mercy and hear us.*
- Take care of our friends and families that are far away from us and keep them safe until we can see them again, we pray. *Have mercy and hear us.*
- Direct our thoughts, feelings, and actions this day and always and help us follow your call, we pray. *Have mercy and hear us.*
- Show those who do not know your love the peace that comes with your name, we pray. *Have mercy and hear us.*
- Raise those who have died and bring them into your everlasting glory, we pray. *Have mercy and hear us.*

Please take time to add your own needs and concerns.

Lord's Prayer

Let us pray in the perfect words
taught to us by Jesus:
Our Father . . .

Closing Prayer

Father of all, you constantly
call us to serve you in the world
around us. Help us always to do
our best to honor you in all we
do and in those we meet. We
ask this through our Lord, Jesus
Christ, your Son, who lives and
reigns with you, in the unity of
the Holy Spirit, one God, forever and ever. Amen.

Dismissal

May the Lord bless us and protect us from evil and bring us to
the joy of heaven. Amen.

Friday, Week 2

Call to Prayer

God, come to my assistance.
Lord, make haste to help me.
Glory to the Father, and to the
    Son, and to the Holy Spirit:
as it was in the beginning, is
    now, and will be forever.
Amen.

Psalm

Antiphon

God will not reject a humble,
sincere heart.

Psalm 51

Have mercy on me, O God,
    according to your steadfast
    love;
according to your abundant
    mercy blot out my transgres-
    sions.
Wash me thoroughly from my
    iniquity,
and cleanse me from my sin.

For I know my transgressions,
and my sin is ever before me.

Against you, you alone, have I
    sinned,
and done what is evil in your
    sight,
so that you are justified in your
    sentence
and blameless when you pass
    judgment.
Indeed, I was born guilty,
a sinner when my mother
    conceived me.

You desire truth in the inward
    being;
therefore teach me wisdom in
    my secret heart.
Purge me with hyssop, and I
    shall be clean;
wash me, and I shall be whiter
    than snow.

Let me hear joy and gladness;
let the bones that you have
    crushed rejoice.
Hide your face from my sins,
and blot out all my iniquities.

Create in me a clean heart, O
    God,
and put a new and right spirit
    within me.
Do not cast me away from your
    presence,

and do not take your holy spirit
from me.

Restore to me the joy of your
salvation,
and sustain in me a willing
spirit.
Then I will teach transgressors
your ways,
and sinners will return to you.

Deliver me from bloodshed, O
God, O God of my salvation,
and my tongue will sing aloud of
your deliverance.
O Lord, open my lips,
and my mouth will declare your
praise.

For you have no delight in
sacrifice;
if I were to give a burnt offering,
you would not be pleased.
The sacrifice acceptable to God
is a broken spirit;
a broken and contrite heart, O
God, you will not despise.

Do good to Zion in your good
pleasure;
rebuild the walls of Jerusalem,
then you will delight in right
sacrifices,
in burnt offerings and whole
burnt offerings;
then bulls will be offered on
your altar.

Glory to the Father, and to the
Son, and to the Holy Spirit:

as it was in the beginning, is
now, and will be forever.
Amen.

Psalm Prayer

Father, see our intention to love
you as sincere and do not reject
us in our weakness. You are the
good news for which we long.

Antiphon

God will not reject a humble,
sincere heart.

Scripture Reading

Ephesians 2:13–16

But now in Christ Jesus you
who once were far off have been
brought near by the blood of
Christ. For he is our peace; in his
flesh he has made both groups
into one and has broken down
the dividing wall, that is, the
hostility between us. He has abol-
ished the law with its commandments and ordinances, that he
might create in himself one new
humanity in place of the two,
thus making peace, and might
reconcile both groups to God in
one body through the cross, thus
putting to death that hostility
through it.

Prayer Response to the Reading

- Listen to us and give us your mercy, because we have sinned.
- Christ Jesus, hear our prayer, because we have sinned.
- Glory to the Father, and to the Son, and to the Holy Spirit.
- Listen to us and give us your mercy, because we have sinned.

Gospel Canticle

Antiphon

Jesus died to bring together all of God's people into one family.

Canticle

- If you are praying in the morning, pray the morning canticle found at the end of chapter 13.
- If you are praying in the evening, pray the evening canticle found at the end of chapter 13.

Glory to the Father, and to the Son, and to the Holy Spirit:
as it was in the beginning, is now, and will be forever. Amen.

Antiphon

Jesus died to bring together all of God's people as one family.

Intercession

Petitions

Jesus, our Savior, has set us free from sin by his sacrifice on the cross and his Resurrection from the dead. Knowing this love for us, we pray: *Have mercy on us, Lamb of God.*

- Watch over your Church and keep it solid in spite of human weaknesses, we pray. *Have mercy on us, Lamb of God.*
- Help us unite ourselves to you in our suffering and pain, and may we feel your closeness during times of difficulty, we pray. *Have mercy on us, Lamb of God.*
- Bring comfort to those who are homeless, penniless, or under hardships of any kind, we pray. *Have mercy on us, Lamb of God.*
- Teach us to help others, even when we are in the middle of troubles and struggles, we pray. *Have mercy on us, Lamb of God.*
- Lead us to an end of all hostilities and wars against one another, we pray. *Have mercy on us, Lamb of God.*

- At the end of our lives, allow us to be with you forever in heaven, we pray. *Have mercy on us, Lamb of God.*

Please take time to add your own needs and concerns.

Lord's Prayer

Let us pray in the perfect words taught to us by Jesus:
Our Father . . .

Closing Prayer

God our Father, the glory of your Son is revealed to us in the suffering he accepted on our behalf. Give us the faith we need to claim as our only goal and need that same cross of our Lord Jesus Christ, your Son, who lives and reigns with you, in the unity of the Holy Spirit, one God, forever and ever. Amen.

Dismissal

May the Lord bless us and protect us from evil and bring us to the joy of heaven. Amen.

Saturday, Week 2

Call to Prayer

God, come to my assistance.
Lord, make haste to help me.
Glory to the Father, and to the
  Son, and to the Holy Spirit:
as it was in the beginning, is
  now, and will be forever.
  Amen.

Psalm

Antiphon

Blessed are you, Virgin Mary,
because you carried the Creator
of the world in your womb.

Psalm 147:12–20

Praise the LORD, O Jerusalem!
Praise your God, O Zion!

For he strengthens the bars of
  your gates;
he blesses your children within
  you.

He grants peace within your borders;
he fills you with the finest of
  wheat.

He sends out his command to
  the earth;
his word runs swiftly.
He gives snow like wool;
he scatters frost like ashes.

He hurls down hail like
  crumbs—
who can stand before his cold?
He sends out his word, and
  melts them;
he makes his wind blow, and the
  waters flow.

He declares his word to Jacob,
his statutes and ordinances to
  Israel.
He has not dealt thus with any
  other nation;
they do not know his ordinances.
Praise the LORD!

Glory to the Father, and to the
  Son, and to the Holy Spirit:
as it was in the beginning, is
  now, and will be forever.
  Amen.

Psalm Prayer

You chose to come to us, O
Word of God, through a humble
servant, the Blessed Virgin Mary.

May we also be willing to bring you into this world by all we say and do.

Antiphon

Blessed are you, Virgin Mary, because you carried the Creator of the world in your womb.

Scripture Reading

Galatians 4:4–5

But when the fullness of time had come, God sent his Son, born of a woman, born under the law, in order to redeem those who were under the law, so that we might receive adoption as children.

Prayer Response to the Reading

- The Lord chose her, the one he loved, from the very beginning.
- He has taken her to live with him forever, from the very beginning.
- Glory to the Father, and to the Son, and to the Holy Spirit.
- The Lord chose her, the one he loved, from the very beginning.

Gospel Canticle

Antiphon

The Lord our God has blessed you, Virgin Mary, above all other women of the world.

Canticle

- If you are praying in the morning, pray the morning canticle found at the end of chapter 13.
- If you are praying in the evening, pray the evening canticle found at the end of chapter 13.

Glory to the Father, and to the Son, and to the Holy Spirit:
as it was in the beginning, is now, and will be forever. Amen.

Antiphon

The Lord our God has blessed you, Virgin Mary, above all other women of the world.

Intercession

Petitions

Let us give thanks to our God, who wished that Mary, the mother of Jesus, be remembered and honored throughout all time. In need, we pray: *May your mother intercede for us, O Word of God.*

- You made Mary the mother of mercy and the mother of us all. May all who face trouble feel her motherly love, we pray. *May your mother intercede for us, O Word of God.*
- You placed Mary as the mother of a family, the home she shared with Joseph and Jesus. Lead all families to reflect this holy model, we pray. *May your mother intercede for us, O Word of God.*
- You strengthened Mary as she waited at the foot of the cross. Give us strength when the struggles of our lives bring us down, we pray. *May your mother intercede for us, O Word of God.*
- You gave Mary the spiritual ears needed to hear your calling. Help us follow her perfect example of listening to you, we pray. *May your mother intercede for us, O Word of God.*
- You have set Mary aside for all time as an example of humble service. Lead us to be humble servants to our friends and families, enemies and strangers, we pray. *May your mother intercede for us, O Word of God.*

- You lifted Mary up to you at the end of her earthly life. May all those who have died rejoice with you and the saints forever, we pray. *May your mother intercede for us, O Word of God.*

Please take time to add your own needs and concerns.

Lord's Prayer

Let us pray in the perfect words taught to us by Jesus:
Our Father . . .

Closing Prayer

All-powerful Father, in Mary we see what is possible for those who love you with their whole hearts. Through her prayers, help us be more like her every day, a person who can change the world. We ask this through our Lord, Jesus Christ, your Son, who lives and reigns with you, in the unity of the Holy Spirit, one God, forever and ever. Amen.

Dismissal

May the Lord bless us and protect us from evil and bring us to the joy of heaven. Amen.

Sunday, Week 3

Call to Prayer

God, come to my assistance.
Lord, make haste to help me.
Glory to the Father, and to the
    Son, and to the Holy Spirit:
as it was in the beginning, is
    now, and will be forever.
    Amen.

Psalm

Antiphon

Praise the name of the LORD.

Psalm 148

Praise the LORD!
Praise the LORD from the
    heavens;
praise him in the heights!
Praise him, all his angels;
praise him, all his host!

Praise him, sun and moon;
praise him, all you shining stars!
Praise him, you highest heavens,
and you waters above the
    heavens!

Let them praise the name of the
    LORD,
for he commanded and they
    were created.
He established them forever and
    ever;
he fixed their bounds, which
    cannot be passed.

Praise the LORD from the earth,
you sea monsters and all deeps,
fire and hail, snow and frost,
stormy wind fulfilling his
    command!

Mountains and all hills,
fruit trees and all cedars!
Wild animals and all cattle,
creeping things and flying birds!

Kings of the earth and all peo-
    ples,
princes and all rulers of the
    earth!
Young men and women alike,
old and young together!

Let them praise the name of the
    LORD,
for his name alone is exalted;
his glory is above earth and
    heaven.

He has raised up a horn for his people,
praise for all his faithful,
for the people of Israel who are close to him.
Praise the LORD!

Glory to the Father, and to the Son, and to the Holy Spirit:
as it was in the beginning, is now, and will be forever.
Amen.

Psalm Prayer

Lord, everything you have created praises you, from the angels in the heavens above to your children in this world. May heaven and earth join their voices to praise you now and for all eternity.

Antiphon

Praise the name of the Lord.

Scripture Reading

1 Peter 1:3–7

Blessed be the God and Father of our Lord Jesus Christ! By his great mercy he has given us a new birth into a living hope through the resurrection of Jesus Christ from the dead, and into an inheritance that is imperishable, undefiled, and unfading, kept in heaven for you, who are being protected by the power of God through faith for a salvation ready to be revealed in the last time. In this you rejoice, even if now for a little while you have had to suffer various trials, so that the genuineness of your faith—being more precious than gold that, though perishable, is tested by fire—may be found to result in praise and glory and honor when Jesus Christ is revealed.

Prayer Response to the Reading

- All of your creation sings of your greatness and glory.
- Timeless is the praise of your greatness and glory.
- Glory to the Father, and to the Son, and to the Holy Spirit.
- All of your creation sings of your greatness and glory.

Gospel Canticle

Antiphon

Go and live the Good News: the Reign of God is here!

Canticle

- If you are praying in the morning, pray the morning canticle found at the end of chapter 13.
- If you are praying in the evening, pray the evening canticle found at the end of chapter 13.

Glory to the Father, and to the Son, and to the Holy Spirit:
as it was in the beginning, is now, and will be forever. Amen.

Antiphon

Go and live the Good News: the Reign of God is here!

Intercession

Petitions

God continues his creation by renewing the world with his love. In this love, we pray: *Renew your creation, O Source of Life.*

- You gave us the Church as a sign of your love for us. Continue to guide those who lead it and your people, we pray. *Renew your creation, O Source of Life.*
- You gave your Son as the ultimate sacrifice for our sins.

May we always do our best to live up to this act of love, we pray. *Renew your creation, O Source of Life.*

- You sent your spirit to strengthen us to do your work. May we use those gifts to benefit those around us, we pray. *Renew your creation, O Source of Life.*
- You show endless patience with your children. May we learn from your example when dealing with our own families and friends, we pray. *Renew your creation, O Source of Life.*
- You give us what we need to survive. Take special care of those who may go without basic needs this day, we pray. *Renew your creation, O Source of Life.*
- You give us everlasting life with you. Bring into your presence forever those who have gone before us, we pray. *Renew your creation, O Source of Life.*

Please take time to add your own needs and concerns.

Lord's Prayer

Let us pray in the perfect words taught to us by Jesus:
Our Father . . .

Closing Prayer

Almighty God, you are our
strength in facing the problems
that will come throughout this
week. Help us live a life that
reflects our moral convictions
and our belief that we are your
children, through your Son,
Jesus Christ, our Lord, who lives
and reigns with you in the unity
of the Holy Spirit, one God, forever and ever.

Dismissal

May the Lord bless us and protect us from evil and bring us to
the joy of heaven. Amen.

Monday, Week 3

Call to Prayer

God, come to my assistance.
Lord, make haste to help me.
Glory to the Father, and to the
    Son, and to the Holy Spirit:
as it was in the beginning, is
    now, and will be forever.
    Amen.

Psalm

Antiphon

Tell the whole world that our
God reigns.

Psalm 96

O sing to the LORD a new song;
sing to the LORD, all the earth.
Sing to the LORD, bless his
    name;
tell of his salvation from day to
    day.

Declare his glory among the
    nations,
his marvelous works among all
    the peoples.
For great is the LORD, and great-
    ly to be praised;

he is to be revered above all
    gods.
For all the gods of the peoples
    are idols,
but the LORD made the heavens.
Honor and majesty are before
    him;
strength and beauty are in his
    sanctuary.

Ascribe to the LORD, O families
    of the peoples,
ascribe to the LORD glory and
    strength.
Ascribe to the LORD the glory
    due his name;
bring an offering, and come into
    his courts.

Worship the LORD in holy splen-
    dor;
tremble before him, all the earth.
Say among the nations, "The
    LORD is king!
The world is firmly established;
    it shall never be moved.
He will judge the peoples with
    equity."

Let the heavens be glad,
and let the earth rejoice;
let the sea roar, and all that fills
    it;

let the field exult, and everything
in it.
Then shall all the trees of the
forest
sing for joy before the LORD;
for he is coming, for he is coming to judge the earth.
He will judge the world with
righteousness,
and the peoples with his truth.

Glory to the Father, and to the
Son, and to the Holy Spirit:
as it was in the beginning, is
now, and will be forever.
Amen.

Psalm Prayer

Nothing is more worthy of our
celebration than all you have
done for us, Lord. May our
praise of you be another sign of
your love to this world.

Antiphon

Tell the whole world that our
God reigns.

Scripture Reading

James 4:11–12

Do not speak evil against one
another, brothers and sisters.

Whoever speaks evil against
another or judges another, speaks
evil against the law and judges
the law; but if you judge the law,
you are not a doer of the law but
a judge. There is one lawgiver
and judge who is able to save
and to destroy. So who, then, are
you to judge your neighbor?

Prayer Response to the Reading

- Only you can help me, Lord,
  because my sins have hurt you.
- Show me your love and mercy
  because my sins have hurt you.
- Glory to the Father, and to
  the Son, and to the Holy
  Spirit.
- Only you can help me, Lord,
  because my sins have hurt you.

Gospel Canticle

Antiphon

Help us in our time of need; just
give the word, and we will have
peace.

Canticle

- If you are praying in the
  morning, pray the morning
  canticle found at the end of
  chapter 13.

- If you are praying in the evening, pray the evening canticle found at the end of chapter 13.

Glory to the Father, and to the Son, and to the Holy Spirit:
as it was in the beginning, is now, and will be forever.
Amen.

Antiphon

Help us in our time of need; just give the word and we will have peace.

Intercession

Petitions

We give you thanks and praise by the good we do. With hearts full of good intentions, we pray: *Help us do what is good, God of all kindness.*

- Continue to guide leaders around the world to actions that are for the benefit of all people, we pray. *Help us do what is good, God of all kindness.*
- Give courage to those who lead your pilgrim Church to stand for the Gospel of life, we pray. *Help us do what is good, God of all kindness.*
- Use us to bring relief to those who are homeless, hungry, and helpless, we pray. *Help us do what is good, God of all kindness.*
- Enlighten our hearts and minds to see you in those around us who may hurt or anger us, we pray. *Help us do what is good, God of all kindness.*
- May we see how much you love us through the love of our families and friends, we pray. *Help us do what is good, God of all kindness.*
- Reward the good of those who have died by granting them life everlasting with you, we pray. *Help us do what is good, God of all kindness.*

Please take time to add your own needs and concerns.

Lord's Prayer

Let us pray in the perfect words taught to us by Jesus:
Our Father . . .

Closing Prayer

God, our Father, we need your
help in our lives now more than
ever. Show us the happiness only
you can provide, while we show
our thanks to you through our
good works. We ask this in the
name of Jesus, your Son, and
in the power of the Holy Spirit.
Amen.

Dismissal

May the Lord bless us and protect us from evil and bring us to
the joy of heaven. Amen.

Tuesday, Week 3

Call to Prayer

God, come to my assistance.
Lord, make haste to help me.
Glory to the Father, and to the
    Son, and to the Holy Spirit:
as it was in the beginning, is
    now, and will be forever.
    Amen.

Psalm

Antiphon

Shine the light of your love upon
us.

Psalm 67

May God be gracious to us and
    bless us
and make his face to shine upon
    us,
that your way may be known
    upon earth,
your saving power among all
    nations.

Let the peoples praise you, O
    God;
let all the peoples praise you.

Let the nations be glad and sing
    for joy,
for you judge the peoples with
    equity
and guide the nations upon
    earth.

Let the peoples praise you, O
    God;
let all the peoples praise you.

The earth has yielded its
    increase;
God, our God, has blessed us.
May God continue to bless us;
let all the ends of the earth revere
    him.

Glory to the Father, and to the
    Son, and to the Holy Spirit:
as it was in the beginning, is
    now, and will be forever.
    Amen.

Psalm Prayer

Bless us, Lord, and shine your
love upon us. Only then can we
be your love in action and serve
you.

Antiphon

Shine the light of your love upon
us.

Scripture Reading

1 John 4:12–15

No one has ever seen God; if we love one another, God lives in us, and his love is perfected in us.

By this we know that we abide in him and he in us, because he has given us of his Spirit. And we have seen and do testify that the Father has sent his Son as the Savior of the world. God abides in those who confess that Jesus is the Son of God, and they abide in God.

Prayer Response to the Reading

- I stand with my God, and my God stands with me.
- I spread the Good News of his Son, and he stands with me.
- Glory to the Father, and to the Son, and to the Holy Spirit.
- I stand with my God, and my God stands with me.

Gospel Canticle

Antiphon

My spirit finds its joy in God.

Canticle

- If you are praying in the morning, pray the morning canticle found at the end of chapter 13.
- If you are praying in the evening, pray the evening canticle found at the end of chapter 13.

Glory to the Father, and to the Son, and to the Holy Spirit:
as it was in the beginning, is now, and will be forever. Amen.

Antiphon

My spirit finds its joy in God.

Intercession

Petitions

Because of the love our God has shown us, we are a people filled with hope. It is with this hope that we pray: *Protect your hopeful people, Lord.*

- Protect, Lord, the Holy Father and the bishops, called to lead and serve, we pray. *Protect your hopeful people, Lord.*
- Protect those who have no one to protect them, those who are persecuted, and those who are in pain, we pray. *Protect your hopeful people, Lord.*

- Protect our hearts from the temptations of everyday life that turn our eyes from you, we pray. *Protect your hopeful people, Lord.*
- Protect the work we do and keep it always pleasing to you, we pray. *Protect your hopeful people, Lord.*
- Guard us from words and actions that hurt those around us, we pray. *Protect your hopeful people, Lord.*
- Protect our friends and family members who have gone to their rest by giving them a place with you in heaven, we pray. *Protect your hopeful people, Lord.*

Please take time to add your own needs and concerns.

Lord's Prayer

Let us pray in the perfect words taught to us by Jesus:
Our Father . . .

Closing Prayer

Merciful God, stay with us, keep us always in your sight, and show us your protective love. Never let us stray from that which makes us truly happy: Jesus Christ, your Son, who lives and reigns with you in the unity of the Holy Spirit, one God, forever and ever. Amen.

Dismissal

May the Lord bless us and protect us from evil and bring us to the joy of heaven. Amen.

Wednesday, Week 3

Call to Prayer

God, come to my assistance.
Lord, make haste to help me.
Glory to the Father, and to the
  Son, and to the Holy Spirit:
as it was in the beginning, is
  now, and will be forever.
  Amen.

Psalm

Antiphon

All the world has seen the love
and power of God.

Psalm 98

O sing to the LORD a new song,
for he has done marvelous
  things.
His right hand and his holy arm
have gotten him victory.

The LORD has made known his
  victory;
he has revealed his vindication in
  the sight of the nations.
He has remembered his steadfast
  love and faithfulness
to the house of Israel.

All the ends of the earth have
  seen
the victory of our God.
Make a joyful noise to the LORD,
  all the earth;
break forth into joyous song and
  sing praises.

Sing praises to the LORD with
  the lyre,
with the lyre and the sound of
  melody.
With trumpets and the sound of
  the horn
make a joyful noise before the
  King, the LORD.

Let the sea roar, and all that fills
  it;
the world and those who live in
  it.

Let the floods clap their hands;
let the hills sing together for joy
  at the presence of the LORD,
for he is coming to judge the
  earth.
He will judge the world with
  righteousness,
and the peoples with equity.

Glory to the Father, and to the
Son, and to the Holy Spirit:
as it was in the beginning, is
now, and will be forever.
Amen.

Psalm Prayer

Gracious God, fill us up with the
love of your name. Then we will
have the strength to go forth and
bring all people closer to you.

Antiphon

All the world has seen the love
and power of God.

Scripture Reading

Ephesians 3:16–21

I pray that, according to the
riches of his glory, he may grant
that you may be strengthened
in your inner being with power
through his Spirit, and that
Christ may dwell in your hearts
through faith, as you are being
rooted and grounded in love.
I pray that you may have the
power to comprehend, with all
the saints, what is the breadth
and length and height and
depth, and to know the love of
Christ that surpasses knowledge,
so that you may be filled with all
the fullness of God.

Now to him who by the
power at work within us is able
to accomplish abundantly far
more than all we can ask or
imagine, to him be glory in the
church and in Christ Jesus to
all generations, forever and ever.
Amen.

Prayer Response to the Reading

- Claim us as your own and
  show us mercy.
- Do not leave us to fend for
  ourselves, and show us mercy.
- Glory to the Father, and to
  the Son, and to the Holy
  Spirit.
- Claim us as your own and
  show us mercy.

Gospel Canticle

Antiphon

Show us mercy, Lord, and
remember the covenant you have
made with us.

Canticle

- If you are praying in the
  morning, pray the morning
  canticle found at the end of
  chapter 13.

- If you are praying in the evening, pray the evening canticle found at the end of chapter 13.

Glory to the Father, and to the Son, and to the Holy Spirit:
as it was in the beginning, is now, and will be forever. Amen.

Antiphon

Show us mercy, Lord, and remember the covenant you have made with us.

Intercession

Petitions

What God can do for us and through us is more than we could ever imagine. Keeping this in mind, we pray: *Gentle Master, help us help one another.*

- Help those who lead your Church to be faithful to you in word and in deed, we pray. *Gentle Master, help us help one another.*
- Help those who do not know the power of your love and are searching for the truth, we pray. *Gentle Master, help us help one another.*

- Help those who are most helpless in this world: children, both born and unborn, the elderly, the sick, and the suffering, we pray. *Gentle Master, help us help one another.*
- Help us always to look for your hand in the good things around us and to be thankful for your blessings, we pray. *Gentle Master, help us help one another.*
- Help us forgive those who have hurt us, misused our trust, or taken us for granted, we pray. *Gentle Master, help us help one another.*
- Help prepare our souls for a place at the heavenly table with those who have gone before us, we pray. *Gentle Master, help us help one another.*

Please take time to add your own needs and concerns.

Lord's Prayer

Let us pray in the perfect words taught to us by Jesus:
Our Father . . .

Closing Prayer

God of mercy and hope, your love for your children is greater than our hearts and minds could know and hold. Help us see and feel that love and spread it to our friends, families, and all those around us, so that all may know the happiness you bring. We ask this through our Lord, Jesus Christ, your Son, who lives and reigns with you in the unity of the Holy Spirit, one God, forever and ever. Amen.

Dismissal

May the Lord bless us and protect us from evil and bring us to the joy of heaven. Amen.

Thursday, Week 3

Call to Prayer

God, come to my assistance.
Lord, make haste to help me.
Glory to the Father, and to the
    Son, and to the Holy Spirit:
as it was in the beginning, is
    now, and will be forever.
    Amen.

Psalm

Antiphon

Come quickly and help your
people.

Psalm 99

The LORD is king; let the peoples
    tremble!
He sits enthroned upon the
    cherubim;
let the earth quake!

The LORD is great in Zion;
he is exalted over all the peoples.
Let them praise your great and
    awesome name.

Holy is he! Mighty King, lover
    of justice,

you have established equity;
you have executed justice and
    righteousness in Jacob.

Extol the LORD our God;
worship at his footstool.
Holy is he!

Moses and Aaron were among
    his priests,
Samuel also was among those
who called on his name.

They cried to the LORD, and he
    answered them.
He spoke to them in the pillar
    of cloud;
they kept his decrees, and the
    statutes that he gave them.

O LORD our God, you answered
    them;
you were a forgiving God to
    them,
but an avenger of their
    wrongdoings.

Extol the LORD our God,
and worship at his holy moun-
    tain;
for the LORD our God is holy.

Glory to the Father, and to the
    Son, and to the Holy Spirit:

as it was in the beginning, is
now, and will be forever.
Amen.

Psalm Prayer

You have power over all your
people, mighty God, but you
gently answer those who call out
to you in faith. Bless us, your
people, and continue to give us
what we truly need.

Antiphon

Come quickly and help your
people.

Scripture Reading

1 Peter 3:8–12

Finally, all of you, have unity
of spirit, sympathy, love for one
another, a tender heart, and a
humble mind. Do not repay evil
for evil or abuse for abuse; but,
on the contrary, repay with a
blessing. It is for this that you
were called—that you might
inherit a blessing. For
"Those who desire life
and desire to see good days,
let them keep their tongues
from evil
and their lips from
speaking deceit;

let them turn away from evil
and do good;
let them seek peace and
pursue it.
For the eyes of the Lord are on
the righteous,
and his ears are open to
their prayer.
But the face of the Lord is
against those who do
evil."

Prayer Response to the Reading

- You satisfy our hungers with
  bread made of the finest
  wheat.
- Give us in your mercy, loving
  God, bread made of the finest
  wheat.
- Glory to the Father, and to
  the Son, and to the Holy
  Spirit.
- You satisfy our hungers with
  bread made of the finest
  wheat.

Gospel Canticle

Antiphon

I am the living bread from heaven. Eat this bread, and you will
live forever.

Canticle

- If you are praying in the morning, pray the morning canticle found at the end of chapter 13.
- If you are praying in the evening, pray the evening canticle found at the end of chapter 13.

Glory to the Father, and to the Son, and to the Holy Spirit:
as it was in the beginning, is now, and will be forever. Amen.

Antiphon

I am the living bread from heaven. Eat this bread, and you will live forever.

Intercession

Petitions

Let us call out to God, our Father in heaven, who feeds his people and watches us with love. With humility, we pray: *Hear your people who hunger.*

- Give faith, hope, and charity to the Pope and all bishops and help them to be models of service, we pray. *Hear your people who hunger.*

- Give those who are open to being converted to the Gospel the will to succeed and the strength from your Holy Spirit to fight on, we pray. *Hear your people who hunger.*
- Give peace of mind and heart to those who are far from the safety of home and family, we pray. *Hear your people who hunger.*
- Give those who want to serve you with good intentions the guidance and wisdom never to wander from your gaze, we pray. *Hear your people who hunger.*
- Give us patience when dealing with our friends and family members who upset us or cause us grief, we pray. *Hear your people who hunger.*
- Give our departed brothers and sisters a place with you in heaven, we pray. *Hear your people who hunger.*

Please take time to add your own needs and concerns.

Lord's Prayer

Let us pray in the perfect words taught to us by Jesus:
Our Father . . .

Closing Prayer

Father, hear the prayer we give you as a gift. In return, feed our hearts and minds with your gifts, so we can live as you want us to live: a people filled with hope and wanting only to serve you. We ask this in the name of Jesus, the Lord, in the power of the Holy Spirit. Amen.

Dismissal

May the Lord bless us and protect us from evil and bring us to the joy of heaven. Amen.

Friday, Week 3

Call to Prayer

God, come to my assistance.
Lord, make haste to help me.
Glory to the Father, and to the
Son, and to the Holy Spirit:
as it was in the beginning, is
now, and will be forever.
Amen.

Psalm

Antiphon

Wash me of my sins, Lord.

Psalm 51

Have mercy on me, O God,
according to your steadfast
love;
according to your abundant
mercy blot out my transgressions.
Wash me thoroughly from my
iniquity,
and cleanse me from my sin.

For I know my transgressions,
and my sin is ever before me.
Against you, you alone, have I
sinned,
and done what is evil in your
sight,
so that you are justified in your
sentence
and blameless when you pass
judgment.
Indeed, I was born guilty,
a sinner when my mother
conceived me.

You desire truth in the inward
being;
therefore teach me wisdom in
my secret heart.
Purge me with hyssop, and I
shall be clean;
wash me, and I shall be whiter
than snow.

Let me hear joy and gladness;
let the bones that you have
crushed rejoice.
Hide your face from my sins,
and blot out all my iniquities.
Create in me a clean heart, O
God,
and put a new and right spirit
within me.
Do not cast me away from your
presence,
and do not take your holy spirit
from me.

Restore to me the joy of your
   salvation,
and sustain in me a willing
   spirit.
Then I will teach transgressors
   your ways,
and sinners will return to you.

Deliver me from bloodshed, O
   God, O God of my salvation,
and my tongue will sing aloud of
   your deliverance.
O Lord, open my lips,
and my mouth will declare your
   praise.

For you have no delight in
   sacrifice;
if I were to give a burnt offering,
   you would not be pleased.
The sacrifice acceptable to God
   is a broken spirit;
a broken and contrite heart, O
   God, you will not despise.

Do good to Zion in your good
   pleasure;
rebuild the walls of Jerusalem,
then you will delight in right
   sacrifices,
in burnt offerings and whole
   burnt offerings;
then bulls will be offered on
   your altar.

Glory to the Father, and to the
   Son, and to the Holy Spirit:
as it was in the beginning, is
   now, and will be forever.
   Amen.

Psalm Prayer

Father, you sent your only Son,
perfect and without sin, into this
world to forgive the sins of your
people. May we continue to do
all we can in our lives to live up
to that incredible gift.

Antiphon

Wash me of my sins, Lord.

Scripture Reading

James 1:2–8

My brothers and sisters, when-
ever you face trials of any kind,
consider it nothing but joy,
because you know that the test-
ing of your faith produces endurance; and let endurance have its
full effect, so that you may be
mature and complete, lacking in
nothing.

   If any of you is lacking in
wisdom, ask God, who gives to
all generously and ungrudgingly,
and it will be given you. But ask
in faith, never doubting, for the
one who doubts is like a wave
of the sea, driven and tossed by
the wind; for the doubter, being
double-minded and unstable in
every way, must not expect to
receive anything from the Lord.

Prayer Response to the Reading

- Christ loves us always and frees us from our sin.
- He feeds us with his body and blood, and frees us from our sin.
- Glory to the Father, and to the Son, and to the Holy Spirit.
- Christ loves us always and frees us from our sin.

Gospel Canticle

Antiphon

What good does it do if you gain all the riches of the world and pay for it with your soul?

Canticle

- If you are praying in the morning, pray the morning canticle found at the end of chapter 13.
- If you are praying in the evening, pray the evening canticle found at the end of chapter 13.

Glory to the Father, and to the Son, and to the Holy Spirit:
as it was in the beginning, is now, and will be forever. Amen.

Antiphon

What good does it do if you gain all the riches of the world and pay for it with your soul?

Intercession

Petitions

We keep our eyes on Christ, our Lord, who came into this world, died, and rose again for us. With this perfect example in our sight, we pray: *Save your people, God of victory.*

- See the good your daughters and sons do for the benefit of others and give them what they need to continue, we pray. *Save your people, God of victory.*
- Continue to call forth leaders and servants for your Church, and give them the courage to answer, we pray. *Save your people, God of victory.*
- Protect us from ourselves, from the actions we do in our daily lives that take us from you, we pray. *Save your people, God of victory.*
- Let us be an example of your love and care to those around us: family, friends, and strangers, we pray. *Save your people, God of victory.*

- Look on the suffering of those in this world who are hurting and suffering through no fault of their own and bless them for it, we pray. *Save your people, God of victory.*
- Lead all souls to heaven, especially those who need your mercy the most, we pray. *Save your people, God of victory.*

Please take time to add your own needs and concerns.

Lord's Prayer

Let us pray in the perfect words taught to us by Jesus:
Our Father . . .

Closing Prayer

Father, you sent Jesus to save your adopted children from themselves. Help us change our lives from something burdened by sin to a sign of your glory and love for all we see. We ask this through the same Jesus Christ, our Lord, and in the power of the Holy Spirit. Amen.

Dismissal

May the Lord bless us and protect us from evil and bring us to the joy of heaven. Amen.

Saturday, Week 3

Call to Prayer

God, come to my assistance.
Lord, make haste to help me.
Glory to the Father, and to the
    Son, and to the Holy Spirit:
as it was in the beginning, is
    now, and will be forever.
    Amen.

Psalm

Antiphon

Blessed are you, Virgin Mary,
because you carried the Creator
of the world in your womb.

Psalm 122

I was glad when they said to me,
"Let us go to the house of the
    LORD!"
Our feet are standing
within your gates, O Jerusalem.

Jerusalem—built as a city
that is bound firmly together.
To it the tribes go up,
the tribes of the LORD,

as was decreed for Israel,
to give thanks to the name of the
    LORD.

For there the thrones for judg-
    ment were set up,
the thrones of the house of
    David.

Pray for the peace of Jerusalem:
"May they prosper who love you.
Peace be within your walls,
and security within your towers."

For the sake of my relatives and
    friends
I will say, "Peace be within you."
For the sake of the house of the
    LORD our God,
I will seek your good.

Glory to the Father, and to the
    Son, and to the Holy Spirit:
as it was in the beginning, is
    now, and will be forever.
    Amen.

Psalm Prayer

The Blessed Virgin Mary did
what you asked her to do, Lord,
and never faltered. For the sake
of your kingdom, for the sake
of our friends and families, and
for the sake of our own salvation, may we follow her perfect
example.

Antiphon

Blessed are you, Virgin Mary, because you carried the Creator of the world in your womb.

Scripture Reading

Revelation 12:1

A great portent appeared in heaven: a woman clothed with the sun, with the moon under her feet, and on her head a crown of twelve stars.

Prayer Response to the Reading

- Holy Mary, mother of God, pray for us sinners.
- Now and at the hour of our death pray for us sinners.
- Glory to the Father, and to the Son, and to the Holy Spirit.
- Holy Mary, mother of God, pray for us sinners.

Gospel Canticle

Antiphon

You received a child from heaven, and you gave birth to the Savior of the world.

Canticle

- If you are praying in the morning, pray the morning canticle found at the end of chapter 13.
- If you are praying in the evening, pray the evening canticle found at the end of chapter 13.

Glory to the Father, and to the Son, and to the Holy Spirit:
as it was in the beginning, is now, and will be forever. Amen.

Antiphon

You received a child from heaven, and you gave birth to the Savior of the world.

Intercession

Petitions

Celebrate Jesus Christ, our Lord, who is the Son of God and the son of Mary. With confidence, we pray: *May your mother intercede for us, our Savior.*

- You gave Mary a share in your saving mission. Strengthen all those who share in this mission today, we pray. *May your mother intercede for us, our Savior.*

- You blessed Mary with the grace to accept all the trials and struggles that came with her calling. Give us the same grace to overcome those trials in our daily lives, we pray. *May your mother intercede for us, our Savior.*
- You lived in this world with Mary and Joseph in a holy family. Help our own families model this beautiful example, we pray. *May your mother intercede for us, our Savior.*
- The servants at the wedding feast followed your words only after your mother told them they should. Open our ears to your words with the help of Mary, we pray. *May your mother intercede for us, our Savior.*
- Your mother witnessed your pain and suffering at the hands of others and never struck back. Help us endure those who hurt us with the same resolve your mother had, we pray. *May your mother intercede for us, our Savior.*
- Mary's reward for her faithfulness and love was a place with you in heaven. Grant this same gift to those who have died, we pray. *May your mother intercede for us, our Savior.*

Please take time to add your own needs and concerns.

Lord's Prayer

Let us pray in the perfect words taught to us by Jesus:
Our Father . . .

Closing Prayer

God, our Father, you set Mary apart from the beginning of time as an example of what we can be if we have faith in your words. Listen to her prayers on our behalf and give us what we need to be faithful and holy as she is faithful and holy. We ask this through our Lord, Jesus Christ, your Son, who lives and reigns with you in the unity of the Holy Spirit, one God, forever and ever. Amen.

Dismissal

May the Lord bless us and protect us from evil and bring us to the joy of heaven. Amen.

Sunday, Week 4

Call to Prayer

God, come to my assistance.
Lord, make haste to help me.
Glory to the Father, and to the
Son, and to the Holy Spirit:
as it was in the beginning, is
now, and will be forever.
Amen.

Psalm

Antiphon

Praise the Lord, for all that he
does is perfect and right.

Psalm 150

Praise the Lord! Praise God in
his sanctuary;
praise him in his mighty
firmament!
Praise him for his mighty deeds;
praise him according to his
surpassing greatness!

Praise him with trumpet sound;
praise him with lute and harp!
Praise him with tambourine and
dance;
praise him with strings and pipe!

Praise him with clanging cymbals;
praise him with loud clashing
cymbals!
Let everything that breathes
praise the Lord!
Praise the Lord!

Glory to the Father, and to the
Son, and to the Holy Spirit:
as it was in the beginning, is
now, and will be forever.
Amen.

Psalm Prayer

Hear the songs of thanks your
people sing to you, Holy God,
and give them what they need
to do the work of the Gospel in
their lives.

Antiphon

Praise the Lord, for all that he
does is perfect and right.

Scripture Reading

2 Timothy 2:8,11–13

Remember Jesus Christ, raised from the dead, a descendant of David—that is my gospel. . . . The saying is sure:

> If we have died with him, we will also live with him;
> if we endure, we will also reign with him;
> if we deny him, he will also deny us;
> if we are faithless, he remains faithful—
> for he cannot deny himself.

Prayer Response to the Reading

- We thank you for your love and faithfulness to us.
- Singing songs of praise and worship for your love and faithfulness to us.
- Glory to the Father, and to the Son, and to the Holy Spirit.
- We thank you for your love and faithfulness to us.

Gospel Canticle

Antiphon

The name of the Lord is praised both on earth and in the heavens.

Canticle

- If you are praying in the morning, pray the morning canticle found at the end of chapter 13.
- If you are praying in the evening, pray the evening canticle found at the end of chapter 13.

Glory to the Father, and to the Son, and to the Holy Spirit:
as it was in the beginning, is now, and will be forever. Amen.

Antiphon

The name of the Lord is praised both on earth and in the heavens.

Intercession

Petitions

Our spirit finds joy and peace in our God, who gives us all good things. With happiness, we pray: *Be our life, O source of life.*

- Give those who lead your Church what they need to be faithful and true to the Gospel, we pray. *Be our life, O source of life.*
- Give food and drink, shelter and clothing, and the peace of your love to those who go without these essentials for human dignity, we pray. *Be our life, O source of life.*
- Give us patience and understanding as we strive to do what is right in dealing with our friends and family, we pray. *Be our life, O source of life.*
- Give all those who seek your ways courage to answer your call, we pray. *Be our life, O source of life.*
- Give hope to all those who cannot feel your presence in their lives, we pray. *Be our life, O source of life.*
- Give the gift of eternal life to those who have gone before us, we pray. *Be our life, O source of life.*

Lord's Prayer

Let us pray in the perfect words taught to us by Jesus:
Our Father . . .

Closing Prayer

Almighty God, help us proclaim your saving power in all we say and do. Enlighten our minds and enkindle our hearts to think and love more like Jesus, your Son, who lives and reigns with you in the unity of the Holy Spirit, one God, forever and ever. Amen.

Dismissal

May the Lord bless us and protect us from evil and bring us to the joy of heaven. Amen.

Monday, Week 4

Call to Prayer

God, come to my assistance.
Lord, make haste to help me.
Glory to the Father, and to the
  Son, and to the Holy Spirit:
as it was in the beginning, is
  now, and will be forever.
  Amen.

Psalm

Antiphon

The God of Light has called
you out of the darkness into the
splendor of light.

Psalm 136:1–9

O give thanks to the LORD,
for he is good,
for his steadfast love endures
  forever.

O give thanks to the God of
  gods,
for his steadfast love endures
  forever.

O give thanks to the Lord of
  lords,

for his steadfast love endures
  forever;

who alone does great wonders,
for his steadfast love endures
  forever;

who by understanding made the
  heavens,
for his steadfast love endures
  forever;

who spread out the earth on the
  waters,
for his steadfast love endures
  forever;

who made the great lights,
for his steadfast love endures
  forever;

the sun to rule over the day,
for his steadfast love endures
  forever;

the moon and stars to rule over
  the night,
for his steadfast love endures
  forever.

Glory to the Father, and to the
  Son, and to the Holy Spirit:
as it was in the beginning, is
  now, and will be forever.
  Amen.

Psalm Prayer

Father, our lives are constantly changing. But your love for us lasts forever. Hear our prayer of praise and grant that we will never turn our backs on your steadfast love.

Antiphon

The God of Light has called you out of the darkness into the splendor of light.

Scripture Reading

1 Thessalonians 3:12–13

And may the Lord make you increase and abound in love for one another and for all, just as we abound in love for you. And may he so strengthen your hearts in holiness that you may be blameless before our God and Father at the coming of our Lord Jesus with all his saints.

Prayer Response to the Reading

- Give thanks to the Lord, for his is a love without end.
- He shows us mercy and compassion, for his is a love without end.

- Glory to the Father, and to the Son, and to the Holy Spirit.
- Give thanks to the Lord, for his is a love without end.

Gospel Canticle

Antiphon

Bless the Lord, who has come to his people and set them free.

Canticle

- If you are praying in the morning, pray the morning canticle found at the end of chapter 13.
- If you are praying in the evening, pray the evening canticle found at the end of chapter 13.

Glory to the Father, and to the Son, and to the Holy Spirit:
as it was in the beginning, is now, and will be forever. Amen.

Antiphon

Bless the Lord, who has come to his people and set them free.

Intercession

Petitions

Because God has proven to be always faithful, we have hope for a future in God's love. Mindful of this, we pray: *Answer your hopeful people.*

- Eternal High Priest, strengthen those who serve the members of your Church on earth, we pray. *Answer your hopeful people.*
- Light to the nations, guide the actions of world leaders and help them do your will, we pray. *Answer your hopeful people.*
- Son of David, bring healing to those who are sick and suffering, we pray. *Answer your hopeful people.*
- Son of Mary, show us how to follow you in faith and trust, we pray. *Answer your hopeful people.*
- Servant of all, help us be like you in our relationships with family and friends—supportive, patient, and forgiving, we pray. *Answer your hopeful people.*
- Risen Lord, grant eternal life to all those who have served you in love and have gone on to their reward, we pray. *Answer your hopeful people.*

Lord's Prayer

Let us pray in the perfect words taught to us by Jesus:
Our Father . . .

Closing Prayer

Father, you are our constant companion, always there to guide our ways. Help us recognize that you are with us in the Scriptures and in the breaking of the bread. We ask this in the name of Jesus, your Son, and in the power of the Holy Spirit. Amen.

Dismissal

May the Lord bless us and protect us from evil and bring us to the joy of heaven. Amen.

Tuesday, Week 4

Call to Prayer

God, come to my assistance.
Lord, make haste to help me.
Glory to the Father, and to the
Son, and to the Holy Spirit:
as it was in the beginning, is
now, and will be forever.
Amen.

Psalm

Antiphon

I can do all things in the name
of the one who has given me
power.

Psalm 144:1–10

Blessed be the LORD, my rock,
who trains my hands for war,
and my fingers for battle;

my rock and my fortress,
my stronghold and my deliverer,
my shield, in whom I take refuge,
who subdues the peoples under
me.

O LORD, what are human beings
that you regard them,
or mortals that you think of
them?
They are like a breath;
their days are like a passing
shadow.

Bow your heavens, O LORD, and
come down;
touch the mountains so that they
smoke.
Make the lightning flash and
scatter them;
send out your arrows and rout
them.

Stretch out your hand from on
high;
set me free and rescue me from
the mighty waters,
from the hand of aliens, whose
mouths speak lies,
and whose right hands are false.

I will sing a new song to you, O
God;
upon a ten-stringed harp I will
play to you,
the one who gives victory to
kings,
who rescues his servant David.

Glory to the Father, and to the Son, and to the Holy Spirit: as it was in the beginning, is now, and will be forever. Amen.

Psalm Prayer

God of power and might, you give us the gifts to fight the evil we encounter. Watch over and protect your people, keeping them safe from harm and ready to do your will.

Antiphon

I can do all things in the name of the one who has given me power.

Scripture Reading

Colossians 3:15–17

And let the peace of Christ rule in your hearts, to which indeed you were called in the one body. And be thankful. Let the word of Christ dwell in you richly; teach and admonish one another in all wisdom; and with gratitude in your hearts sing psalms, hymns, and spiritual songs to God. And whatever you do, in word or deed, do everything in the name of the Lord Jesus, giving thanks to God the Father through him.

Prayer Response to the Reading

- Turn to the Lord, your God, with your whole heart, and he will cleanse you of your sins.
- Show a heart that is humble and repentant, and he will cleanse you of your sins.
- Glory to the Father, and to the Son, and to the Holy Spirit.
- Turn to the Lord, your God, with your whole heart, and God will cleanse you of your sins.

Gospel Canticle

Antiphon

God comes from heaven above to save his people.

Canticle

- If you are praying in the morning, pray the morning canticle found at the end of chapter 13.

- If you are praying in the evening, pray the evening canticle found at the end of chapter 13.

Glory to the Father, and to the Son, and to the Holy Spirit:
as it was in the beginning, is now, and will be forever. Amen.

Antiphon

God comes from heaven above to save his people.

Intercession

Petitions

We thank Christ, our Lord, who gives the people of God strength and power to journey toward heaven. With confidence, we pray: *Protect your pilgrim people, Christ, our Shepherd.*

- Continue to send courageous leaders to your Church on earth, ministers to lead and serve your children, we pray. *Protect your pilgrim people, Christ, our Shepherd.*
- Bless and protect those who are most in need, the unborn, the sick, and those who have no one to stand up for them,

we pray. *Protect your pilgrim people, Christ, our Shepherd.*
- Keep us safe and free from the temptations in our daily lives that lead us from your love, we pray. *Protect your pilgrim people, Christ, our Shepherd.*
- See our love for you in the good we try to do and forgive us for those times we may hurt others or ourselves, we pray. *Protect your pilgrim people, Christ, our Shepherd.*
- Take special care of those around us, our family, friends, and strangers, who make your love present to us in what they say and do, we pray. *Protect your pilgrim people, Christ, our Shepherd.*
- Reward with eternal life those who have completed their earthly pilgrimages, we pray. *Protect your pilgrim people, Christ, our Shepherd.*

Please take time to add your own needs and concerns.

Lord's Prayer

Let us pray in the perfect words taught to us by Jesus:
Our Father . . .

Closing Prayer

God, our Father, you sent your
Son to us as the ideal we all long
to be. In him, you have adopted
us as your own sons and daughters. Help the words we say and
the actions we take match the
love we hold in our hearts. We
ask this in the name of Jesus, the
Lord, in the unity of the Holy
Spirit. Amen.

Dismissal

May the Lord bless us and protect us from evil and bring us to
the joy of heaven. Amen.

Wednesday, Week 4

Call to Prayer

God, come to my assistance.
Lord, make haste to help me.
Glory to the Father, and to the
   Son, and to the Holy Spirit:
as it was in the beginning, is
   now, and will be forever.
   Amen.

Psalm

Antiphon

Those who put their trust in
God know what true happiness
is.

Psalm 146

Praise the LORD!
Praise the LORD, O my soul!
I will praise the LORD as long as
   I live;
I will sing praises to my God all
   my life long.

Do not put your trust in princes,
in mortals, in whom there is no
   help.
When their breath departs, they
   return to the earth;

on that very day their plans per-
   ish.

Happy are those whose help is
   the God of Jacob,
whose hope is in the LORD their
   God,
who made heaven and earth,
the sea, and all that is in them;

who keeps faith forever; who
   executes justice for the
   oppressed;
who gives food to the hungry.
The LORD sets the prisoners free;
the LORD opens the eyes of the
   blind.

The LORD lifts up those who are
   bowed down;
the LORD loves the righteous.
The LORD watches over the
   strangers;
he upholds the orphan and the
   widow,

but the way of the wicked he
   brings to ruin.
The LORD will reign forever,
   your God,
O Zion, for all generations.
Praise the LORD!

Glory to the Father, and to the
Son, and to the Holy Spirit:
as it was in the beginning, is
now, and will be forever.
Amen.

Psalm Prayer

The only way to find the happiness we long for is to place our trust in you, LORD. Keep our eyes always fixed on you and our hearts open to your love.

Antiphon

Those who put their trust in God know what true happiness is.

Scripture Reading

1 John 2:3–6

Now by this we may be sure that we know him, if we obey his commandments. Whoever says, "I have come to know him," but does not obey his commandments, is a liar, and in such a person the truth does not exist; but whoever obeys his word, truly in this person the love of God has reached perfection. By this we may be sure that we are in him: whoever says, "I abide in him," ought to walk just as he walked.

Prayer Response to the Reading

- My heart is ready, O God, my heart is ready.
- Because I have come to know you and listen to your words, my heart is ready.
- Glory to the Father, and to the Son, and to the Holy Spirit.
- My heart is ready, O God, my heart is ready.

Gospel Canticle

Antiphon

Lord, I love to listen to your word.

Canticle

- If you are praying in the morning, pray the morning canticle found at the end of chapter 13.
- If you are praying in the evening, pray the evening canticle found at the end of chapter 13.

Glory to the Father, and to the Son, and to the Holy Spirit:
as it was in the beginning, is now, and will be forever.
Amen.

Antiphon

Lord, I love to listen to your word.

Intercession

Petitions

Jesus is the Word of God, and his message is Good News for all people. Thankful for this gift, we pray: *Hear us, Word of God.*

- Watch over those who shepherd the Church, our Holy Father and the bishops, the descendants of the Apostles, and keep them true to the Gospel, we pray. *Hear us, Word of God.*

- Make us mindful of our own words, words that can hurt or words that can heal, and guide our thoughts and speech, we pray. *Hear us, Word of God.*

- Your word brings peace to those who hear it. Send it to those places of violence and unrest that need it the most, we pray. *Hear us, Word of God.*

- With only a word, you healed the sick among you. Bring comfort and relief to those in our lives who are ailing in body or spirit, we pray. *Hear us, Word of God.*

- You forgave those who tried to harm you with words of hate. Give us the wisdom to forgive others as you did, we pray. *Hear us, Word of God.*

- You have the words of everlasting life. Grant this to our brothers and sisters who have died, we pray. *Hear us, Word of God.*

Please take time to add your own needs and concerns.

Lord's Prayer

Let us pray in the perfect words taught to us by Jesus:
Our Father . . .

Closing Prayer

God, you raised up a fallen world by sending your Son as our redeemer. Open our hearts to his words and forgive us when we do not listen. We ask this in the name of our Lord, Jesus Christ, your Son, who lives and reigns with you in the unity of the Holy Spirit, one God, forever and ever. Amen.

Dismissal

May the Lord bless us and protect us from evil and bring us to the joy of heaven. Amen.

Thursday, Week 4

Call to Prayer

God, come to my assistance.
Lord, make haste to help me.
Glory to the Father, and to the
    Son, and to the Holy Spirit:
as it was in the beginning, is
    now, and will be forever.
    Amen.

Psalm

Antiphon

The Lord rebuilds Jerusalem and
heals the brokenhearted.

Psalm 147:1–11

Praise the LORD!
How good it is to sing praises to
    our God;
for he is gracious,
and a song of praise is fitting.

The LORD builds up Jerusalem;
he gathers the outcasts of Israel.
He heals the brokenhearted,
and binds up their wounds.

He determines the number of
    the stars;
he gives to all of them their
    names.
Great is our Lord, and abundant
    in power;
his understanding is beyond
    measure.

The LORD lifts up the
    downtrodden;
he casts the wicked to the
    ground.
Sing to the LORD with
    thanksgiving;
make melody to our God on the
    lyre.

He covers the heavens with
    clouds,
prepares rain for the earth,
makes grass grow on the hills.
He gives to the animals their
    food,
and to the young ravens when
    they cry.

His delight is not in the strength
    of the horse,
nor his pleasure in the speed of
    a runner;
but the LORD takes pleasure in
    those who fear him,
in those who hope in his stead-
    fast love.

Glory to the Father, and to the
  Son, and to the Holy Spirit:
as it was in the beginning, is
  now, and will be forever.
  Amen.

Psalm Prayer

God, our Father, you know the
number of the stars in the sky,
because your life-giving hand
placed them there. Heal our
broken hearts, gather us into one
people, and bless us with your
wisdom and grace.

Antiphon

The Lord rebuilds Jerusalem and
heals the brokenhearted.

Scripture Reading

Romans 8:18–21

I consider that the sufferings of
this present time are not worth
comparing with the glory about
to be revealed to us. For the
creation waits with eager longing
for the revealing of the children
of God; for the creation was subjected to futility, not of its own
will but by the will of the one
who subjected it, in hope that
the creation itself will be set free
from its bondage to decay and
will obtain the freedom of the
glory of the children of God.

Prayer Response to the Reading

- Blessed are the people who
  have put their faith in God,
  the Savior.
- The sufferings of the present
  time will be nothing to the
  people who have put their
  faith in God, the Savior.
- Glory to the Father, and to
  the Son, and to the Holy
  Spirit.
- Blessed are the people who
  have put their faith in God,
  the Savior.

Gospel Canticle

Antiphon

I am the way, the truth, and the
life; no one comes to the Father
unless it is through me.

Canticle

- If you are praying in the
  morning, pray the morning
  canticle found at the end of
  chapter 13.

- If you are praying in the evening, pray the evening canticle found at the end of chapter 13.

Glory to the Father, and to the Son, and to the Holy Spirit:
as it was in the beginning, is now, and will be forever. Amen.

Antiphon

I am the way, the truth, and the life; no one comes to the Father unless it is through me.

Intercession

Petitions

We pray to Christ, the light of the world and the joy of all creation, as we say: *Lead us to glory by your light.*
- Watch over your Church and help those who are called to lead it to be faithful and joy-filled people, we pray. *Lead us to glory by your light.*
- Shine your light over all the earth, so that every person may hear your name and know the wonders of your love, we pray. *Lead us to glory by your light.*

- Bring us out of the darkness brought on by our own sin and weakness, we pray. *Lead us to glory by your light.*
- Make us an example of your glory to all we encounter, family and friends, strangers and enemies, we pray. *Lead us to glory by your light.*
- Take care of those who are homeless, penniless, and in need of the joy of your presence, we pray. *Lead us to glory by your light.*
- Grant eternal rest to our departed brothers and sisters, and may your perpetual light shine upon them, we pray. *Lead us to glory by your light.*

Please take time to add your own needs and concerns.

Lord's Prayer

Let us pray in the perfect words taught to us by Jesus:
Our Father . . .

Closing Prayer

Father, let the knowledge of your love enlighten our hearts and minds and allow us to serve you fearlessly and freely, giving you the glory that is due. We ask this through our Lord, Jesus Christ, your Son, who lives and reigns with you in the unity of the Holy Spirit, one God, forever and ever. Amen.

Dismissal

May the Lord bless us and protect us from evil and bring us to the joy of heaven. Amen.

Friday, Week 4

Call to Prayer

God, come to my assistance.
Lord, make haste to help me.
Glory to the Father, and to the
    Son, and to the Holy Spirit:
as it was in the beginning, is
    now, and will be forever.
    Amen.

Psalm

Antiphon

Deliver me from bloodshed,
God of my salvation.

Psalm 51

Have mercy on me, O God,
    according to your steadfast
    love;
according to your abundant
    mercy blot out my transgres-
    sions.
Wash me thoroughly from my
    iniquity,
and cleanse me from my sin.

For I know my transgressions,
and my sin is ever before me.

Against you, you alone, have I
    sinned,
and done what is evil in your
    sight,
so that you are justified in your
    sentence
and blameless when you pass
    judgment.
Indeed, I was born guilty,
a sinner when my mother
    conceived me.

You desire truth in the inward
    being;
therefore teach me wisdom in
    my secret heart.
Purge me with hyssop, and I
    shall be clean;
wash me, and I shall be whiter
    than snow.

Let me hear joy and gladness;
let the bones that you have
    crushed rejoice.
Hide your face from my sins,
and blot out all my iniquities.

Create in me a clean heart, O
    God,
and put a new and right spirit
    within me.
Do not cast me away from your
    presence,

and do not take your holy spirit
from me.

Restore to me the joy of your
salvation,
and sustain in me a willing
spirit.
Then I will teach transgressors
your ways,
and sinners will return to you.

Deliver me from bloodshed, O
God, O God of my salvation,
and my tongue will sing aloud
of your deliverance.
O LORD, open my lips,
and my mouth will declare your
praise.

For you have no delight in
sacrifice;
if I were to give a burnt offering,
you would not be pleased.
The sacrifice acceptable to God
is a broken spirit;
a broken and contrite heart, O
God, you will not despise.

Do good to Zion in your good
pleasure;
rebuild the walls of Jerusalem,
then you will delight in right
sacrifices,
in burnt offerings and whole
burnt offerings;
then bulls will be offered on
your altar.

Glory to the Father, and to the
Son, and to the Holy Spirit:

as it was in the beginning, is
now, and will be forever.
Amen.

Psalm Prayer

Father, you sent your sinless Son
to save us and bring us back to
you. Ease the stress we feel on
our troubled hearts and help us
find our way back to you.

Antiphon

Deliver me from bloodshed,
God of my salvation.

Scripture Reading

Galatians 2:16,19–20

Yet we know that a person is
justified not by the works of the
law but through faith in Jesus
Christ. And we have come to
believe in Christ Jesus, so that
we might be justified by faith
in Christ, and not by doing the
works of the law, because no one
will be justified by the works of
the law. . . . For through the
law I died to the law, so that I
might live to God. I have been
crucified with Christ; and it is
no longer I who live, but it is
Christ who lives in me. And the
life I now live in the flesh I live
by faith in the Son of God, who

loved me and gave himself for me.

Prayer Response to the Reading

- To you, my Lord, I make my prayer for mercy.
- Hear me, I have sinned against you.
  I make my prayer for mercy.
- Glory to the Father, and to the Son, and to the Holy Spirit.
- To you, my Lord, I make my prayer for mercy.

Gospel Canticle

Antiphon

Give your people knowledge of salvation and forgive our sins.

Canticle

- If you are praying in the morning, pray the morning canticle found at the end of chapter 13.
- If you are praying in the evening, pray the evening canticle found at the end of chapter 13.

Glory to the Father, and to the Son, and to the Holy Spirit:. as it was in the beginning, is now, and will be forever. Amen.

Antiphon

Give your people knowledge of salvation and forgive our sins.

Intercession

Petitions

Our mighty Savior is the source of all hope for those who know the power of his name. Humbly, we pray: *Have mercy and hear our prayer.*

- Renew your holy Church and help its leaders and members walk in the light of hope, we pray. *Have mercy and hear our prayer.*
- Give world leaders the foresight to make decisions that will benefit all of your people, we pray. *Have mercy and hear our prayer.*
- Do not judge us by the wrongs we have done but by the good we long for in our hearts, we pray. *Have mercy and hear our prayer.*

- Show your compassionate love to those who are oppressed and in danger and give them safety and peace, we pray. *Have mercy and hear our prayer.*
- Use us to spread your mercy and hope to those we meet, we pray. *Have mercy and hear our prayer.*
- Give pardon and peace to those who have died and place them with your saints in heaven, we pray. *Have mercy and hear our prayer.*

Please take time to add your own needs and concerns.

Lord's Prayer

Let us pray in the perfect words taught to us by Jesus:
Our Father . . .

Closing Prayer

Eternal Father, without you we can do nothing. Help our selfishness die and help us live a new life with Jesus at the center. We ask this in his name, in unity with the Holy Spirit. Amen.

Dismissal

May the Lord bless us and protect us from evil and bring us to the joy of heaven. Amen.

Saturday, Week 4

Call to Prayer

God, come to my assistance.
Lord, make haste to help me.
Glory to the Father, and to the
Son, and to the Holy Spirit:
as it was in the beginning, is
now, and will be forever.
Amen.

Psalm

Antiphon

Blessed are you, Mary ever virgin, for you carried the eternal
Word of God in your womb.

Psalm 115

Not to us, O LORD, not to us,
but to your name give glory,
for the sake of your steadfast love
and your faithfulness.
Why should the nations say,
"Where is their God?"
Our God is in the heavens; he
does whatever he pleases.

Their idols are silver and gold,
the work of human hands.

They have mouths, but do not
speak;
eyes, but do not see.

They have ears, but do not hear;
noses, but do not smell.
They have hands, but do not
feel;
feet, but do not walk;

they make no sound in their
throats.
Those who make them are like
them;
so are all who trust in them.

O Israel, trust in the LORD!
He is their help and their shield.
O house of Aaron, trust in the
LORD!
He is their help and their shield.

You who fear the LORD, trust in
the LORD!
He is their help and their shield.
The LORD has been mindful of
us;

he will bless us; he will bless the
house of Israel;

he will bless the house of Aaron;
he will bless those who fear the
LORD,
both small and great.

May the LORD give you increase,
both you and your children.
May you be blessed by the
LORD,
who made heaven and earth.

The heavens are the LORD's
heavens,
but the earth he has given to
human beings.
The dead do not praise the
LORD,
nor do any that go down into
silence.

But we will bless the LORD
from this time on and forevermore.
Praise the LORD!

Glory to the Father, and to the
Son, and to the Holy Spirit:
as it was in the beginning, is
now, and will be forever.
Amen.

Psalm Prayer

The Virgin Mary blessed your
name, mighty Lord, by her will-
ingness to do what you asked of
her. May we bless your name by
doing all that you ask us to do.

Antiphon

Blessed are you, Mary ever virgin, for you carried the eternal
Word of God in your womb.

Scripture Reading

Romans 8:29–30

For those whom he foreknew
he also predestined to be con-
formed to the image of his Son,
in order that he might be the
firstborn within a large family.
And those whom he predestined
he also called; and those whom
he called he also justified; and
those whom he justified he also
glorified.

Prayer Response to the Reading

- We share in the fruit of life
  through you, chosen daughter
  blessed by the Lord.
- You humbly accepted your
  role in the divine plan, chosen
  daughter blessed by the Lord.
- Glory to the Father, and to
  the Son, and to the Holy
  Spirit.
- We share in the fruit of life
  through you, chosen daughter
  blessed by the Lord.

Gospel Canticle

Antiphon

I am the servant of the Lord. Let
it be done according to your will.

Canticle

- If you are praying in the morning, pray the morning canticle found at the end of chapter 13.
- If you are praying in the evening, pray the evening canticle found at the end of chapter 13.

Glory to the Father, and to the Son, and to the Holy Spirit:
as it was in the beginning, is now, and will be forever. Amen.

Antiphon

I am the servant of the Lord. Let it be done according to your will.

Intercession

Petitions

Jesus, our Savior, chose to come into the world through the Virgin Mary and set her apart for all time. Knowing this to be true, we pray: *May your mother intercede for us, Lord.*

- Mary answered the angel's call with a humble and sincere heart. Help the Church on earth to follow her timeless example and listen when you call, we pray. *May your mother intercede for us, Lord.*

- With the help of Joseph, Mary raised you in a loving and holy family. May families today work to become more holy and loving, we pray. *May your mother intercede for us, Lord.*

- Mary walked with you on the road to Calvary and suffered with you at the foot of your cross. Help us endure our own pain and anguish with the same resolve and grace, we pray. *May your mother intercede for us, Lord.*

- After your death, the disciple whom you loved took in Mary. May we take care of those around us in our own families who are in need, we pray. *May your mother intercede for us, Lord.*

- You gave Mary as a mother to your disciple and to us. Help us live lives worthy of such a noble and holy woman, we pray. *May your mother intercede for us, Lord.*

- Mary sits as Queen of Heaven, ready to greet those who have gone before us in faith. May they see her face and all the saints at the heavenly banquet, we pray. *May your mother intercede for us, Lord.*

Please take time to add your own needs and concerns.

Lord's Prayer

Let us pray in the perfect words taught to us by Jesus:
Our Father . . .

Closing Prayer

Heavenly Father, you take the common and make it uncommon. By coming to your people through the Blessed Virgin Mary, you set her apart from all others, and the child she bore was the Savior of us all. May the common actions of our lives become uncommon and special by your grace and our faith in your love. We ask this in the name of Jesus, the Lord, in unity with the Holy Spirit. Amen.

Dismissal

May the Lord bless us and protect us from evil and bring us to the joy of heaven. Amen.

Morning Canticle

The Canticle of Zechariah: Luke 1:68–79

Blessed be the Lord God of Israel,
because he has visited his people with deliverance,
and has raised for us a horn of salvation
in the house of David, his servant.

As he promised throughout past ages,
in the words of his holy prophets:
deliverance from our enemies,
and from the control of our oppressors.

He has shown kindness to our ancestors,
remembering always his holy covenant.
The oath sworn to Abraham, our father,
he has renewed for us.

So that, freed from the clutches of our foes,
we may serve him without fear,
becoming holy and just in his sight
the rest of our days.

And you, child called 'prophet of the Most High,'

will go before the Lord, to prepare his ways,
bringing his people knowledge of
salvation,
through remission of their sins.

For the love of our compassionate God,
as the Orient on high has shown
upon us
to illumine the darkness and dis-
pel the shadow of death,
to direct our steps along peaceful
ways.

Glory to the Father, and to the
Son, and to the Holy Spirit:
as it was in the beginning, is
now, and will be forever.
Amen.

Evening Canticle

The Canticle of Mary:
Luke 1:46–55

My soul proclaims the greatness
of the Lord,
my spirit rejoices in God my
Savior
for he has looked with favor on
his lowly servant.

From this day all generations
will call me blessed:
the Almighty has done great
things for me,
and holy is his Name.

He has mercy on those who fear
him
in every generation.
He has shown the strength of
his arm,
he has scattered the proud in
their conceit.

He has cast down the mighty
from their thrones,
and has lifted up the lowly.
He has filled the hungry with
good things,
and the rich he has sent away
empty.

He has come to the help of his
servant Israel
for he has remembered his
promise of mercy,
the promise he made to our
fathers,
to Abraham and his children for
ever.

Glory to the Father, and to the
Son, and to the Holy Spirit:
as it was in the beginning, is
now, and will be forever.
Amen.

Acknowledgments

The scriptural quotations contained herein are from the New Revised Standard Version of the Bible, Catholic Edition. Copyright © 1993 and 1989 by the Division of Christian Education of the National Council of the Churches of Christ in the United States of America. All rights reserved.

The prayers, devotions, beliefs, and practices contained herein have been verified against authoritative sources.

The material labeled *Catechism* is from the English translation of the *Catechism of the Catholic Church* for use in the United States of America. Copyright © 1994 by the United States Catholic Conference, Inc.—Libreria Editrice Vaticana. Used with permission.

The prayer by Saint Alphonsus Liguori on page 39; the prayer by Saint Francis de Sales on page 41; the "Prayer of Saint Catherine of Siena" on page 41; "Three Prayers of Saint Ignatius of Loyola" on pages 41–42; the "Prayer of Saint Gertrude the Great" on page 42; the prayer by Saint Padre Pio on pages 45–46 and the prayer by Saint Augustine of Hippo on page 46 are from The Feast of All Saints Web site, at *www.feastofsaints.com/index.htm,* accessed July 15, 2007.

The "Prayer of Saint Francis of Assisi," by Saint Francis of Assisi, on page 46 is found at *www.catholicforum.com/saints/pray0027.htm,* accessed October 1, 2005.

The quotation and prayer on page 55 are from *The Icon: Window on the Kingdom,* by Michael Quenot (Crestwood, NY: Saint Vladimir's Seminary Press, 1991), pages 12 and 13. Copyright © 1991 by Saint Vladimir's Seminary Press. Used with permission.

The prayer "The Road Ahead" on pages 59–60 is from *Thoughts in Solitude,* by Thomas Merton (New York: Farrar, Straus, Cudahy, 1956, 1986), page 83. Copyright © 1958 by the Abbey of Our Lady of Gethsemani. Copyright renewed 1986 by the trustees of the Thomas Merton Legacy Trust. Used with permission of Farrar, Straus and Giroux, LLC.

The words of Saint Josephine Bakhita on page 65 are from "Black Catholics: Josephine Bakhita," on the National Black Catholic Congress Web site, at *www.nbccongress.org/black-catholics/black-saints-saint-josephine-bakhita.asp,* accessed Juuly 15, 2007.

The prayers on pages 67, 67, 71, 71–72, 72, and 73 are from *Prayer Without Borders: Celebrating Global Wisdom,* edited by Barbara Ballenger (Baltimore, MD: Catholic Relief Services, 2004), pages 29, 47, 93, 101, 49, and 31, respectively. Copyright © 2004 by Catholic Relief Services. Used with permission.

The prayers "Light a Holy Fire" and "Father, Thank You" on page 68 are from *An African Prayer Book,* selected by Desmond Tutu (New York: Walker and Company, 1995), pages 128 and 65–66. Copyright © 1995 by Desmond Tutu. Used with permission of Doubleday, a division of Random House, Inc.

"The Wayfarer's Prayer" on page 72 is from *Companion of Hopes: Prayers for Migrant Youth,* by the Youth and Migration Program of the Mexican Commission of Youth Ministry, as quoted in *Prayer Without Borders: Celebrating Global Wisdom,* page 51.

The prayer by Dom Helder Camara on pages 73–74 is quoted in *Prayer Without Borders: Celebrating Global Wisdom,* pages 44–45. Copyright © by Dom Helder Camara Institute.

The section "Praying as a Poem" on pages 77–79 is from the *Teaching Activities Manual for "The Catholic Youth Prayer Book,"* by Rebecca Rushing (Winona, MN: Saint Mary's Press, 2006), handout 8–B. Copyright © 2006 by Saint Mary's Press. All rights reserved.

The section "The Four R's of *Lectio Divina*" on pages 85–89 is adapted from *Catechetical Sessions on Christian Prayer,* by Laurie Delgatto and Mary Shrader (Winona, MN: Saint Mary's Press, 2004), pages 95–96. Copyright © 2004 by Saint Mary's Press. All rights reserved.

The guided meditation on pages 94–97 is adapted from "Baptism: This Is My Beloved Child," in the leader's guide for *Guided Meditations for Youth on Sacramental Life,* by Jane E. Arsenault and Jean R. Cedor (Winona, MN: Saint Mary's Press, 1993), pages 11–17. Copyright © 1993 by Saint Mary's Press. All rights reserved.

The "Journaling" chapter on pages 99–105 and the "Personal Salvation History" sidebar on page 100 are adapted from *PrayerWays,* by Carl Koch (Winona, MN: Saint Mary's Press, 1995), pages 91–93 and 94. Copyright © 1995 by Saint Mary's Press. All rights reserved.

The excerpts and quotation by Pope John Paul II on pages 113, 115, and 118 are from "Constitution on the Sacred Liturgy *Sacrosanctum Concilium"* solemnly promulgated by His Holiness Pope Paul VI on December 4, 1963, numbers 11, 48, and 2, respectively, at *www.vatican.va/archive/hist_councils/ ii _vatican_council/documents/vat-ii_const_19631204_sacrosanctum-concilium _en.html,* accessed July 15, 2007.

The prayers on page 114 are from the English translation of *The Roman Missal* © 2010, International Commission on English in the Liturgy (ICEL). All rights reserved.

Endnote Cited in a Quotation from the *Catechism of the Catholic Church*

1. Cf. *Romans* 8:29; Council of Trent (1547): Denzinger-Schönmetzer, *Enchiridion Symbolorum, definitionum et declarationum de rebus fidei et morum* (1965) 1609–1619.

Endnotes Cited in Quotations from "Constitution on the Sacred Liturgy" *Sacrosanctum Concilium*

1. Cf. 2 Cor. 6:1.
2. Cf. St. Cyril of Alexandria, Commentary on the Gospel of John, book XI, chap XI–XII: Migne, Patrologica, 74, 557–564.

Art Credit

Snark/Art Resource, NY: page 51

Notes

Notes

Notes

Notes